The

A Christian–Muslim Dialogue

A record of the seminar 'Building Bridges' held
at Lambeth Palace, 17–18 January 2002

Edited by Michael Ipgrave

CHURCH HOUSE
PUBLISHING

Church House Publishing
Church House,
Great Smith Street,
London SW1P 3NZ

ISBN 0 7151 5002 2
GS Misc 672

Published 2002 by Church House Publishing

Cover design by Church House Publishing
Typeset in Stone Serif 10pt
Printed by The Cromwell Press, Trowbridge, Wiltshire

Contents

Participants in the
Christian–Muslim seminar
Lambeth Palace
17–18 January 2002

Mr Raficq Abdulla
Kingston University

Professor Leila Ahmed
Harvard University

Dr Seyed Amir Akrami
*Organisation for Islamic Culture
and Communication, Tehran*

Dr Rabiatu Ammah
University of Ghana

His Holiness Aram I
Catholicos of Cilicia

Professor Mehmet Aydin
University of Izmir

Dr Zaki Badawi
The Muslim College, London

The Revd Professor Michael
Banner
King's College London

The Most Revd and Rt Hon.
Dr George Carey
Archbishop of Canterbury

His Eminence Dr Mustafa Cerić
*Grand Mufti of Bosnia and
Herzegovina*

Professor Vincent Cornell
University of Arkansas

The Rt Revd Kenneth Cragg
*Assistant Bishop in the Diocese
of Oxford*

Dr Mohamed El-Awa
*Egyptian Society for Culture
and Dialogue*

Mrs Heba Raouf Ezzat
Cairo University

The Rt Revd Michael Fitzgerald
*Pontifical Council for Inter-
Religious Dialogue, and Bishop
of Nepte*

Professor David Ford
Cambridge University

Professor Yvonne Haddad
Georgetown University

His Royal Highness Prince El
Hassan bin Talal
Jordan

The Rt Revd Josiah Idowu-Fearon
Bishop of Kaduna

The Revd Dr Michael Ipgrave
*Adviser on Inter Faith Relations to
the Archbishops' Council, Church
of England*

Dr Asma Jahangir
Advocate, Supreme Court of Pakistan

Mr Hamid Kasiri
University of Innsbruck

Professor David Kerr
Edinburgh University

Professor Tarif Khalidi
Cambridge University

Dr Philip Lewis
University of Bradford

Professor Tarek Mitri
World Council of Churches, Geneva

Mr Sohail Nakhooda
Amman

Professor Azim Nanji
Institute of Ismaili Studies, London

The Rt Revd Dr Michael Nazir-Ali
Bishop of Rochester

Professor Jorgen Nielsen
Birmingham University

Dr Farhan Nizami
Oxford Centre for Islamic Studies

Professor Tariq Ramadan
College of Geneva and *University
of Fribourg*

Dr Justice Nasim Hasan Shah
Chief Justice of Pakistan (retired)

Dr Mona Siddiqui
Glasgow University

The Most Revd Henri Teissier
Archbishop of Algiers

The Revd Dr David Thomas
Birmingham University

Dr Christian Troll SJ
*Phil.-Theol. Hochschule St Georgen,
Frankfurt am Main*

Professor Frances Young
Birmingham University

Facilitator
Professor Gillian Stamp
*The Brunel Institute of
Organisational and Social Studies*

Introducing the seminar

The Most Revd and Rt Hon. Dr George Carey,
Archbishop of Canterbury

His Royal Highness Prince El Hassan bin Talal of Jordan

The Rt Hon. Tony Blair, The Prime Minister

The Most Revd and Rt Hon. Dr George Carey, Archbishop of Canterbury

On 17 and 18 January 2002 some forty Muslim and Christian scholars gathered in a historic place for a historic purpose. Lambeth Palace, which has been home to Archbishops of Canterbury for over eight hundred years, has seen its fair share of remarkable gatherings since the twelfth century. In my own time as Archbishop there have been several occasions that might qualify for that description – but none more so, I suspect, than the seminar that I was privileged to host for those two days.

We came from many different countries and from a variety of traditions and backgrounds, bringing with us at least one thing in common: a strong commitment to deepen the dialogue and to broaden the understanding and cooperation between our two great faiths – Christianity and Islam. Of course, it would be wrong to suggest that this was an entirely new departure. Indeed it is a road more and more travelled in recent years and many of the participants were already experienced wayfarers.

However, it also has to be acknowledged that the events of September 11 2001 and their aftermath gave fresh impetus and focus to the shared journey of Christians and Muslims. Those events also highlighted the importance of deepening our dialogue and understanding, not just for the sake of our own faith communities, but also for the well-being and security of the world. There is a widespread sense of urgency about drawing on the rich resources of our faith traditions to challenge those who claim God's blessing for the evil they do and the hatred they preach. So, although we met as theologians and religious scholars, we did so in the certain knowledge that our work could have resonance and value way beyond our gathering.

We had much to discuss over our two days together. We spoke of God and of God's purposes for the human family; we spoke of the history of our communities, and how they have interacted; we spoke of life in community, the good society and how it is shaped by faith; we reflected on the challenges of the modern world and of the questions which we must face in our dialogue.

And what did we achieve? A simple answer, a deceptively simple one perhaps, is: greater understanding. I believe that in the course of our discussions and informal conversations significant bridges were built, which I hope and pray will facilitate further dialogue in the years to come. I believe that we also went on our way recognizing more fully than before our responsibilities as religious leaders and scholars to help our communities live together in ways which do not suppress our own identities but open us up to the riches which the other offers. We were reminded that we owe it to those communities, as they stand today and as they will be in the future, to do all we can to confront that challenge with all our heart and mind. That will involve trying to help our own faith communities overcome suspicion and apprehension – and yes, at times, hatred and intolerance. We also face the serious challenge that there are many around us who believe that the world would be better off without faith and all its apparent capacity to generate division, hatred and violence. So we must play our part in trying to ensure that the wider world may reap the best – not fear the worst – of what our faiths have to offer.

I conclude with words which I addressed to the opening session of the seminar – words which also serve as an invitation to all who read this record of a significant and hopeful gathering of Muslims and Christians:

> So let us now approach this encounter daring to believe that God has drawn us together. In neither of our faiths is God a subject of idle intellectual curiosity. We are concerned with the living, loving God who brought all things into being and who seeks to bring his creation to its proper fulfilment, with the human family living together in justice and peace. It is this God whose guidance we seek and whose glory we serve.

His Royal Highness
Prince El Hassan bin Talal
of Jordan

A few years after the end of the Cold War, Samuel Huntington theorized that the clash of political ideologies that it had represented would be replaced by a 'clash of civilizations', in which religious and cultural differences would become the new criteria in distinguishing a dangerous 'other'. The two sides to the conflict would still be East and West, albeit with this difference: 'East' would no longer signify the Soviet Union, but a particular view of Islam – an Islam opposed by a 'West' representative less of a triumphant Christendom than of a secular 'modernity.'

Because of the controversy generated by this thesis – not only in the rarefied realm of academia, but also in the tangible world, in which even academics must live – there has been much talk of the necessity of dialogue between civilizations aimed at addressing past, present and future misunderstandings and preventing Huntington's 'clash'. Yet, while I am prepared to offer my unqualified support to the underlying sentiment, I must dispute the notion that the current dialogue is between civilizations.

It can only be between cultures. The word 'civilization' actually refers to culture; to a society's cultural achievements in acquiring knowledge and developing technology. It may also be defined as 'the culture characteristic of a particular time or place'. However, although the world was once large enough to foster several civilizations simultaneously, both time and space have been dramatically compressed by the modern revolution in technology. Today, there is only one civilization: one that encompasses all cultures.

Civilization has always been a cumulative process; for although the earliest ones seemingly withered away, only to be replaced by a successor or successors, historians tell us that they usually merged or regenerated themselves to arise in new forms. The measure of their greatness lay in their willingness to borrow from predecessors and contemporaries and to be enriched by their own constituent cultures. Difference was not seen as a threat, but as a reality; it was not a route to degeneration, but to renewal. Stagnation, decline and oblivion were the consequences when dominant cultures spurned the opportunity for constant forward motion through cooperation, interaction and adaptation. For, much like people, societies must absorb and internalize new knowledge before they elaborate upon it and evolve. But while individuals can survive without evolving, societies cannot. So although we now share one common civilization, founded upon mutual respect rather than domination, we must not consign its constituent cultures to stagnation, decline and oblivion.

Today, we still hear loose references to civilization in the context of religion, as in 'Christian civilization' and 'Islamic civilization', the implication being that some sort of dichotomy exists – that the two are mutually exclusive and necessarily contradictory, or even antagonistic. Yet these 'civilizations' are actually metaphors for the civilizing power of faith. Anyone may join them; for belief is the only criterion for membership. As universal religions, neither of these 'civilizations' may be circumscribed by time or place, or made redundant by their compression. They represent two different expressions of the same 'civilizational' values; two different interpretations of the same eternal trusts. Thus, both may be present in the same society without risk of contradiction and both may be present in the same world without risk of confrontation.

But confrontation is the danger that we face at this juncture in history, dominated as it is by a culture of war. It is the culture of war that is the real contradiction; for it directly opposes our shared beliefs and values. If we believe in free will, can we say that there is no alternative? If we believe in equality, can we say that some are more equal than others? If we believe in justice, can we say that terror and might are the arbiters?

If our civilization fails to uphold the values underlying it, particularly in the most adverse circumstances, then those values become meaningless and hollow, and civilization itself becomes an object of derision. Instead of moving forward and evolving, we will slide backwards into barbarity and social disintegration. Before that happens, we must recognize that we need one another, that we need to learn about one another and that, even in our ignorance, we enrich and inspire one another.

The history of Christian–Muslim dialogue shows us that progress is made when representatives of both faiths put aside differences in theology and rite in order to concentrate upon areas of agreement, particularly moral values and ethical principles. Yet, dogmatism is not the preserve of religion, but is a very human trait found across the cultural spectrum. Perhaps the civilizing power of faith provides us with a means to reinforce mutual respect, avoid misunderstanding and deadlock, and de-escalate the tensions that lead to pointless confrontations. Perhaps mercy and compassion are not just attributes that we assign to God, but humanitarian values upon which we must act if we are to show that we are truly civilized.

It was within that spirit that we met as Christians and Muslims in dialogue at Lambeth. This collection of papers points both to the values that we hold in common and to the challenges that we must face together.

The Rt Hon. Tony Blair, MP, The Prime Minister

We live in an unprecedented era, an era of a highly connected world, increasingly interdependent as globalization links up economies, individuals and ideas. We know far more about each other than our ancestors did, and increasingly we find ourselves face to face with people of radically different values and world-views.

On the one hand, this globalization process is making possible, for the first time in history, the emergence of some genuinely global, shared values of tolerance and respect, even as our societies become more intermixed and therefore diverse. But, on the other hand, we have to recognize too that change, especially change as fast moving as the process of globalization, can produce fears and tensions – and these we cannot ignore. People come up against the unfamiliar and that can be disconcerting.

Now humankind is perfectly capable of adapting to change. Societies have constantly adapted and renewed themselves in response to massive change. But I believe that if we are to adapt successfully to these changes – the changes of more contact, faster communication, more interaction across cultures – then we must be willing to learn more about each other's history, traditions and faiths. Knowledge dispels fear. Knowledge clears away misunderstanding. Knowledge strengthens trust.

That search for greater knowledge must embrace our different beliefs as well. For belief is at the very heart of societies, of different cultures, shaping them day by day, year by year, over the centuries. However secular some of our societies seem to have become, they remain informed by centuries of faith.

And if that is so – if belief is central to society – we must achieve a better understanding of each other's beliefs if we are all to live in harmony in this fast-changing world. We must share our experiences of the transcendent, of what it means to be people of faith in today's societies, of how communities adapt to change.

Together we have to grapple with some of the challenges that those changes present us with. Those challenges include the ethical, the theological, and the legal. And I am glad that the Christian–Muslim seminar at Lambeth Palace in January this year explored how these two great religions have faced those challenges and can continue to do so.

We need religions to engage with each other and with society, to find solutions to many difficult questions: questions of social justice, of ethics, of peace. Such a dialogue, while contributing to the common good, will also displace fear and engender the confidence that the other's wisdom is not a threat, but enriches common understanding.

As members of the one human family and as believers, Christians and Muslims have obligations to the common good, to justice and to solidarity. Religions can work to this end each informed by its own tradition – but with a commitment to the harmony of the whole.

Religious dialogue does not have to deny or trivialize differences, but it should look at the common elements in faith, as well as trying to understand the differences. It should acknowledge that there is far more that unites than divides; far more that enables than disables. It is dialogue between persons that helps to make us who we are – yet we do not lose our personal distinctiveness. As Christians and Muslims we can and should know and respect the religious convictions of the other, to discover the similarities and the differences.

What are those similarities? A belief in community; a belief in justice; a belief in the dignity of the human person; a belief that a world without values would be an empty place. Both Christians and Muslims worship a living God, merciful and almighty, the creator of heaven and earth, who has also spoken to people on this earth. Both submit themselves to the hidden decrees of God, just as Abraham submitted himself to God's plan. Muslims, although not acknowledging him as God, venerate Jesus as a prophet.

For us all, God's name must be identified with peace and tolerance. Seminars such as the one this book records show us that dialogue between faiths can be based on openness to other believers, a willingness to listen and the desire to respect and understand others in those differences. This does not result in the erosion of differences or the creation of one religion, but it allows believers to share and learn from one another.

I am aware that there are also those who say that we cannot live together in a pluralistic community of faiths. But neither history nor reality would agree with that. Earlier centuries benefited greatly from the cross-fertilization of ideas. For example, the great medieval thinker St Thomas Aquinas was anxious to learn from Islamic philosophers.

On my trips to the Middle East, I have seen at first hand the reality which has lasted for many centuries of Christians and Muslims living in harmony.

Christians and Muslims, I believe, can live, work and flourish together. This can only work if we accept our differences and show each other respect. Without that tolerance and respect, we show the world religion at its worst – and I believe we do a fundamental disservice to God. A community of believers founded on principles of tolerance and respect will be a more credible sign of hope to humanity.

Editorial preface

The structure of the Lambeth seminar was built around five pairs of scholars (each consisting of one Muslim and one Christian), each presenting a pair of papers on one of the five general themes identified in the five chapter headings of this volume. In the first four sessions, each paper was followed by a prepared response (from a scholar of the other faith to the presenter), leading into a general discussion. In the final session, following reflections by Bishop Michael Nazir-Ali and Professor Gillian Stamp on the process to date, participants split into small groups to offer their suggestions for ways of carrying the dialogue forward in the future.

The chapters that follow contain edited versions of the ten papers and two final reflections, together with notes based on two of the responses that were in effect short presentations on specific subjects. The rest of the material is my summary of the other responses (attributed by name to the respondents), together with an indication of the main points made in discussion (unattributed) and brief introductory material for each chapter. The postscript, 'Ways ahead', draws together some of the suggestions for future work made in the small groups.

In compiling this material, I have been greatly helped by comments from a number of the participants, and particularly by the wise advice of the Revd Canon Dr David Marshall. As distinct from the papers given by participants, though, all the summary material has been compiled by me, and I take full responsibility for any inadvertent misunderstanding or omission of individual participants' views that may have occurred.

A short glossary of some technical terms appearing in the text is included (pp. 121–5).

Michael Ipgrave

Acknowledgements

The publisher gratefully acknowledges permission to reproduce copyright material in this publication. Every effort has been made to trace and contact copyright holders. If there are any inadvertent omissions we apologize to those concerned and will ensure that a suitable acknowledgement is made at the next reprint. Numbers in parentheses indicate page numbers in this publication.

Faber & Faber: Extract fom T. S. Eliot, 'The Journey of the Magi' (1937), in *Collected Poems*, 1909–1962 (Faber, 1975), p. 110 (113).

'Story Water' (16 lines) from The *Essential Rumi* by Rumi, translated by Coleman Barks with John Moyne, A.J. Arberry and Reynold Nicholson (Penguin Books, 1999). Copyright © Coleman Barks, 1995. (116)

Building bridges between Christians and Muslims

Michael Ipgrave

On 17 and 18 January 2002, forty Muslim and Christian scholars from around the world met at Lambeth Palace, the London home of the Archbishop of Canterbury, for a two-day seminar to discuss issues in Christian–Muslim relations. This volume presents a record of that seminar – edited versions of the twelve papers which were presented, and a distillation of the responses and discussions which followed.

The gathering hosted by the Archbishop was truly international in character. HRH Prince El Hassan bin Talal of Jordan was joined by Muslim scholars from ten other countries, including six from the United Kingdom; Christian participants came from eight countries. This range was important in ensuring that the discussion was focused on the relations of 'Muslims and Christians', rather than 'Islam and the West'. The latter is the rhetorical framework – sometimes expressed in terms of a 'clash of civilizations' – within which much debate has taken place recently, particularly since September 11 2001. The involvement in this dialogue of both Muslims living in the West and non-Western Christians is a reminder of the inadequacy of any such simplistic approach. Certainly the attacks on New York and Washington, and all that has followed since then in Afghanistan and elsewhere, were never far from the minds of seminar participants; nor was the continuing situation in Israel–Palestine. There was a recognition from everybody, though, that these issues cannot be addressed by Christians and Muslims aligning their faiths on either side of a supposedly global fault-line. The aim must be, rather, to explore how these two monotheistic religions can contribute to finding solutions rather than perpetuating problems, and – as a first step towards that – to create an environment in which some of the obstacles to mutual understanding could be overcome.

This is, in one sense, a task of 'building bridges', as the seminar's title expressed it: creating routes for information, appreciation and respect to travel freely and safely in both directions between Christians and Muslims, Muslims and Christians. The seminar at Lambeth was widely regarded by participants and others as a bridge-building project of both significance and considerable potential. It had a special symbolic resonance because of its location, and because of the support given to the project by the British Prime Minister, and the encouragement lent by his presence at the opening of the event. It is of course not the only such project under construction, and would not want to be seen in that light; an energy for meeting, dialogue and interaction is in evidence in the field of shared Christian–Muslim endeavour.

As well as 'building bridges', though, the record which follows shows also a sense of occupying common ground – inhabiting a certain *terra media*, as Prince Hassan put it. This is not just a question of Muslims and Christians communicating with one another across a barrier, but also of finding that in some ways we are already standing alongside one another in today's world. This is in no way to devalue the distinctiveness, and at times the irreducible differences, that mark out our beliefs, our practices, our attitudes and our histories; many of the papers and discussions which follow devote considerable attention precisely to acknowledging, delineating and even affirming what has been called 'the dignity of difference'. However, there is also a clear awareness that people of both faiths face the imperative and the opportunity of working together to address shared challenges in our diverse societies and in our common world. Some of these are specifically concerned with relations between Christians and Muslims, but others involve people of other faiths also, and all need to reckon with the realities of secularity. Nobody wants Christian–Muslim interaction to proceed in an exclusive way which shuts out these wider dimensions of engagement.

The papers and responses collected in this book follow the pattern of the seminar, which sought to cover a very wide range of issues in Christian–Muslim relations from the perspective of the current situation of our two faiths.

Chapter 1 'Christians and Muslims face to face' seeks to give an overall orientation on the place of the two faiths, relative to one other, to the world, and to God.

Chapter 2 'Learning from history' adds to this the depth of more than a thousand years of interaction, asking how the varied experiences of the past can inform the present and future.

Chapter 3 'Communities of faith' explores some of the problems and opportunities that both religious communities face in a pluralistic world.

Chapter 4 'Faith and change', sets out the challenges which major transformations in societies pose to both religions, and looks at some of the ways Christianity and Islam have responded.

Chapter 5 'Setting the agenda', must be read as in an important sense unfinished, since its completion will rely on the initiative and commitment of far wider circles of Christians and Muslims than those who gathered at Lambeth.

After reviewing some of the themes and processes of the seminar, and examining the dynamics of Christian–Muslim interaction in regional and global contexts, the book ends by gathering together some suggestions for fruitful ways ahead to pursue in the future. Much that is good and creative is in fact already happening, from individual and family friendships, through neighbourhood and city-wide projects for dialogue and cooperation, to national and global initiatives. Such examples of good practice can help to fill out the suggestions emerging from this seminar, which of necessity are rather general in character.

At the same time, it may be that the mapping out of common ground, the respectful acknowledgement of difference, and the firm commitment to future collegiality that these pages express can give some hope and encouragement to Christians and Muslims who are engaged in the issues in practical ways. For me personally, two messages stand out clearly from all that follows: first, that there is an enormous and pressing task of mutual education facing both our communities; and second, that we firmly believe that the God to whom we witness is calling us to engage more deeply and trustfully with one another for the sake of his world.

Chapter 1

Christians and Muslims face to face

How are we to understand the context within which Muslims and Christians encounter one another today? The sense of a 'face to face' meeting is certainly valuable, in that it speaks of the directness, honesty and trust with which people of the two faiths should enter into dialogue with one another. Yet this is only part of the overall dynamic of Christian–Muslim meeting, and taken in isolation there is the danger that it could suggest an attitude of confrontation or even belligerence. There are several other dimensions which are needed realistically to fill out the 'face to face' imagery. In the first place, in many parts of the world – for example, the Middle East or South Asia, and to some extent also Western Europe – there are other significant religious traditions to reckon with, such as Judaism, Hinduism, Sikhism or Buddhism. Then again, both Christianity and Islam have to take account of the complex and contentious issue of 'the secular', however that is to be understood. Most importantly of all, both Christians and Muslims are fundamentally oriented towards the face of God:

> My soul thirsts for God, the God of life; when shall I go to seek the face of God?[1]

> To God belong the East and the West; whithersoever you turn, there is the Face of God.[2]

Dialogue between Christians and Muslims needs to take account not only of social and historical dynamics, but also of the theological implications of two faiths both of which see themselves as centred in God. The two papers in this chapter develop different aspects of this multi-faceted context of encounter. In the first, **Grand Mufti Dr Mustafa Cerić**, through an overview of religious and cultural relations between the two faiths with special reference to Europe, proposes a shift from the habit of critically judging one another to the shared project of 'designing value'. Next, **Bishop Kenneth Cragg** brings the insights of a theological and dialogical reading of Qur'anic texts to bear on questions of religion and secularity in the contemporary world. The two papers invite discussion on a number of points – the interface of religions and cultures, the relative weighting of similarities and differences between the two faiths, the limits of human autonomy and accountability.

Remembering the past, thinking the present, dreaming the future

Mustafa Cerić

Assimilation and isolation

In one of his stories, Paulo Coelho tells of a task assigned by a wise man to a boy who seeks the secret of happiness. The man asks him to walk around a palace for two hours holding a teaspoon with two drops of oil, which he must be careful not to spill. On his return, the boy is asked what he has seen; he has to confess that, in his concern not to spill the oil, he noticed nothing. Again the wise man sends him out, telling him to observe his surroundings. The boy returns this time full of the wonders of the palace – but in his inattention he has spilt the oil. The wise man explains that the secret of happiness is 'to see all the marvels of the world, and never to forget the drops of oil on the spoon'.[3]

This little story illustrates the human temptation towards either of two equally precarious ends: assimilation or isolation. If we forget faith in our hearts, we risk losing the sense of our identity, but if we close our eyes before the marvels of the world's cultures, we become lonely islands without a clear purpose.

This question of assimilation or of isolation of one's faith, to the extent of either becoming like someone else without recognition, or of becoming detached from other things or persons with a selfish attitude, does not pertain only to one religion or culture, but to all religions and cultures. In particular though, it concerns Islam and Christianity. It is similarity, rather than diversity, between Christianity and Islam that makes their followers sometimes close to, sometimes far from one another.

Monotheism: logic and perception

The doctrine of monotheism is shared by Islam and Christianity, but the perception of it seems unsettling, not because of the lack of an apodictic argument but because of a dispute conducted in an *ad hominem* manner. Muslims refrain from the Christian doctrine of the

Trinity, while Christians withhold recognition of the Muslim doctrine of the finality of Muhammad's prophethood. By emphasizing the doctrine of the Trinity, Muslims believe that Christianity is failing to maintain the purity of monotheism. On the other hand, by insisting on the finality of Muhammad's prophethood, Christians believe that Islam is not appreciating the historical centrality of Jesus. So, the issue here is not a matter of logic, but rather of emotions based on perception. It is only if perception changes that emotions change, because logic does not change emotions.

Cooperation: the right way

It is, then, the fear of being perceived to become like the other, i.e. of being assimilated in one's religion or culture, that makes some people tend to religious or cultural isolation. I am not sure that this fear can be overcome by a theatrical dialogue, whether religious or otherwise. I am certain, though, that a meaningful dialogue, which nourishes Muslim–Christian interaction and cooperation as against both cultural assimilation and religious isolation, is an imperative strongly founded on the experience of the past, a momentum of the present, and something for which there can be no alternative in the future. The time has come to open up the process of combining diverse parts into the complex whole of a Muslim–Christian past, present and future. There is a need to bring Christian and Muslim communities into equal membership of a common society – and this is especially important for those groups or persons previously discriminated against on religious, racial or cultural grounds.

Muslim–Christian cooperation should not be seen as an act of assimilation, but an equal opportunity accompanied by cultural diversity in an atmosphere of mutual tolerance. For I believe that neither the weak nor the aggressive will inherit the earth, but the cooperative.

From interaction to cooperation: positive examples from the past

Of course, there is no cooperation without interaction. Physics teaches that there are four distinct types of force through which the manifold transformations of matter and energy arise – strong, electromagnetic, weak, and gravitational interactions. I believe that we can find in religions and cultures equivalent forces, through which manifold transformations of mind and spirit may arise as a result of the interactions of the strong and the weak, the influential and the gravitational.

It was due to Muslim–Christian interactions in the fields of philosophy, theology, mathematics, chemistry, astronomy, medicine, architecture and literature, as well as trade and travel, that the mind and spirit of Europe was able to be transformed into the rationality of the Renaissance, marking the transition from medieval to modern times.

If, as has been said, language does not lie, we may easily discover the fruits of Muslim–Christian interactions in the past by observing how many English words have Arabic or Islamic roots – *admiral, algebra, algorithm, azimuth, calibre, chemistry, cotton, gala, mafia, mattress, sugar, traffic, zenith, zero*, and so on.[4]

The benefit of Muslim–Christian interactions in the past could be further illustrated by reference to some of the Muslim scientists whose books one could have found on Europe's bookshelves in the fifteenth century and beyond: Abd al-Aziz al-Qabisi ('Alchabitius', d. 967) on astronomy,[5] al-Battani ('Albetegnius', d. 929) on mathematics,[6] ibn Sina ('Avicenna', 980–1037) on medicine,[7] al-Razi ('Rhasis' or 'Rhazes', d. 924) on natural science,[8] ibn Haytham ('Alhazen the Younger', 965–1038) on physics,[9] or Jabir ibn Hayyan ('Gaber', fl. 775) on technology.[10]

These illustrations show the results of the second historic interaction and cooperation between Islam and Christianity, whereby for medieval Christians classical knowledge and the wisdom of other cultures was filtered through the minds of Muslim believers in One God. However, one should not forget that the first interaction was that whereby for Muslims the earlier Christian and Hebrew writers smoothed the path for the initiation of the Eastern 'Hakeem man'[11] as a precursor of the Western 'Renaissance man'. Both 'Hakeem man' and 'Renaissance man' excelled in many skills and fields of knowledge, but most important of all was that they knew how to 'see all the marvels of the world, and never to forget the drops of oil on the spoon'. They were both true representatives of their respective traditions – Islam and Christianity – and genuine scholars, artists, writers, innovators and scientists. They felt no need to hide either their religious or cultural identity. Their communication was honest and direct, without mediator or arbiter.

Wrong mediators

Unfortunately, this kind of communication between Islam and Christianity has somehow been lost long since to different mediators and arbiters, either for the sake of proclaimed modernity, or for sake of political conformity. Thus we have now a third wave of interaction between Islam and Christianity, which can be described as telling more what Islam and Christianity should not be rather than what they are and what they should be in a process of self-examination and self-actualization in today's history. Ordinary Muslims and Christians cannot be entirely free from blame for the intrusion of these wrong mediators and arbiters into their mutual affairs, since they proved unable to free themselves from the old negative habits of judging one another.

With due respect to his capability as a writer, Salman Rushdie is an illustrative example of an assimilated Muslim in the West who uses Eastern wisdom to demonstrate his Western modernity. Nevertheless, Rushdie has in fact achieved nothing, because the modernity he wants to demonstrate is not his, and the eastern wisdom he uses is not true. Hence, he has become precisely the wrong mediator between Muslim East and Christian West, in the sense of both betraying the true spirit of the East and deceiving the honest audience of the West.

Similarly, as the Bosnian writer (and winner of the Herder Prize) Dzevad Karahasan[12] has observed, the phenomenon of Osama bin Laden is 'a typical example of the mentality of the modern man in using the modern technology and mass-media'. Therefore, bin Laden became the 'Wrong man' of the East and the 'Wanted man' of the West. He opted for isolation in the East, using the tools of modern technology to probe the logic of the might of the modern world. Of course, bin Laden too has proven nothing except his ignorance of the true spirit of past interactions, present cooperation, and future relations between Islam and Christianity. He is just another example of a fake arbiter between Islam and Christianity, arising from the lack of honest and direct interaction and cooperation between Christians and Muslims in their religious as well as their cultural identities.

Europe: a continent of many faiths

Honest interaction and cooperation between Christians and Muslims is especially important for Europe because in its self-understanding Europe has been perceived as a 'Christian continent'. Yet this perception is incorrect. It is a fact of history that throughout the centuries large communities of Jewish and Muslim people have lived in Europe. From the Iberian to the Balkan peninsula, these two communities have made important contributions to European life and culture. All three monotheistic religions – Judaism, Christianity and Islam – arrived at Europe from the East and were welcomed by European people at certain times and for different reasons. Thus, Europe has always been a continent of many faiths. It is of course true that the arrival of Islam on the European continent was not appreciated by all, but the same could also be said of Christianity, which had to make its way through heavy storms of disapproval before it finally found its place in the European mind. The drama of European life and culture was a series of events involving an interesting and intense conflict of different forces, even before the coming of the idea of Islam as a way of life and a specific driving force of history. The Muslim–Christian meeting with Europe was one of the most interesting and most intense competitive actions in the history of the continent. In some cases, this competition was an affirmative action; in others, it involved an opposition of needs, drives, wishes, external or internal demands.

What matters is the fact that Christianity and Islam could not ignore each other any more, but had to count on one another in their sense of self-examination and self-actualization. On one hand, for example, it certainly was not the sword of ibn Sina ('Avicenna', 980–1037) that made St Thomas Aquinas (1224–1274) take him as his master in theology and philosophy, but rather the force of ibn Sina's Islamic spirit that challenged Thomas to examine and to actualize the spirit of Christianity. On the other hand, it was an opposition of drives, external and internal demands that caused Dante Alighieri (1265–1321) to wish that ibn Rushd ('Averroes', 1126–1198) should go to hell because of his promotion of Aristotelian philosophy.

The difference between these two approaches lies in the fact that Thomas knew how to value Avicenna's philosophy, not to judge it, while Dante jumped to a judgement of 'Averroism', so displaying poetic emotions rather than sound perception. It is only if perception changes that emotions change, because logic does not change emotions. Moreover, a judgemental approach is based on reflecting past reality, and has no energy for designing new realities. We may discover the truth, but we need to design value. This is exactly what Thomas Aquinas shows by reflecting on the philosophy of Avicenna – he designed new philosophical value out of Avicenna's thought, which is as Aristotelian as it was and as Islamic as it meant to be.

Qur'anic guidance

It is in the spirit of designing rather than judging that I interpret this verse of the Qur'an:

> To you, Muhammad, the Book has been sent in truth, confirming the Scripture that came before it, and protecting it in safety: so judge between them by what God has revealed, and follow not their vain desires, diverging from the Truth that has come to you. To each among you a Law has been prescribed and an Open Way. If God had so willed, He would have made you a single People, but He wanted to test you in what He has given you: so compete as in a race in all values. The goal of you all is to God; it is He that will show you the truth of the matters in which you dispute.[13]

There are two important points that should be taken from this Qur'anic teaching. First, we are to adopt an inclusive, not an exclusive approach, to the worlds of faith. This is especially important for Europe, because Europe's future will be one of many faiths. It is, therefore, necessary to overcome our history of intolerance of the other's scripture, i.e. of the religion of others. Second, the Qur'an guides us to the conclusion that no one has the monopoly on Truth. The road to Truth is open to all, and the way to it is through competition in good virtues and in the design of new values of human decency, righteousness and knowledge.

How are we to change our judgement habits? – since without judgement we would spend time, effort and energy figuring things out each time. Judgement is about recognizing the meaning and symbols of the other and our own. Is it then possible for us to design a new symbol to indicate that our social interactions are in no sense predatory? The purpose of design is to move forward, while habits of judgement keep us stuck in one place, or direct us backward. Habits of design open new opportunities, providing a logic that is not only a tool for thinking or a mechanism for communication mechanism, but a logic of dia-logic.

Intentionally or not, Muslims and Christians have ceased to communicate with each other directly because they could not free themselves from old habits of judgement, and thus have been left out of the new design of a world that has consigned them to either active isolation or passive assimilation. The part of social, cultural and religious integration has thus been taken away from both Christians and Muslims who claim the authority of the scripture. Not only have they ceased to trust each other on the basis of their scriptures, but they have also lost trust in meaningful communication with those who claim to design for them a 'meaningful mediation'.

Religious identity

Old patterns of religious identity were dismissed as 'irrational', and a new and 'normal' identity was understood to be either derived from liberal individualism or from class. Marxism left memories of a class identity, with a notion of economic determinism that was supposed to erase the identity of individual freedom, in particular the freedom of religion. On the other hand, liberal individualism has failed to comprehend the power of identity politics, assuming that the defeat of Fascism and Nazism was a final blow to extreme nationalism. Since the eighteenth century, Europe has thus been faced with a dilemma of political power being based on either reason or on identity. Yet this is a false dilemma, because it has been proven that these two do not necessarily exclude each other. In the words of George Schöpflin:

> In essence, recourse to reason provides clarity in understanding action, consistency, accountability, predictability, the ability to question motives and place them in a frame of reference. Identity, as against this, offers individuals the security of community and solidarity, of shared patterns of meanings, a bounded world in which to live and in which one can find others like oneself. Power operates in both these spheres. The exclusion of either reason or identity creates unease.[14]

Religion is one of the factors that make up personal and group identities. The question is how religious identity can be saved from misuse to legitimate other issues and instead be used to motivate people to strive for peace, justice and tolerance in everyday life situations. Today, we do not live in separate worlds of our own. Within a relatively short period of history, telephone, radio, television, motion pictures, and more recently computers, e-mail, and the World Wide Web are drastically altering our perceptions of time, space and each other. However, these tools of modern technology, though connecting people closer to each other in a physical sense, do not bear fruit in making them closer in the sense of decent human relationships. From Northern Ireland to the Middle East, centuries of bloody ethnic and religious conflicts continue to be far from peaceful resolution. The tragic events in New York and Washington are the culmination of this human madness. I have tried to show the inevitability of remembering positive historic interactions between Muslims and Christians in the past, so that both Christians and Muslims may recognize that their present interactions should lead them to a future cooperation based on mutual respect, equality and worth.

European Muslim, Muslim European

I am an authentic European Muslim as much as I am a traditional Muslim European from the Balkan peninsula. Unfortunately, my brothers and sisters from the Iberian peninsula were not able to survive the history of Europe. Nevertheless, Europe is my history and destiny, my home and my future. I hope that it is a bright one, full of meaningful interactions and cooperation among all Europeans – Christians, Muslims, Jews and others who appreciate the rhythm of European life.

It is my dream that Europe shall recognize and accept my Islamic identity in accordance with the real spirit of its democracy and human rights. Indeed, my dream is to live in Europe as a genuine European as I am a genuine Muslim. Therefore, any hostility towards European values of democracy and human rights disturbs me as much as any prejudice against Islam and Muslims.

My dream is that my homeland Bosnia be free, safe, democratic and prosperous in Europe, and that never again will the European people to whom I belong by my faith, nationality and culture experience the pain of Srebrenica.

My dream is that a united Europe will live in peace and security with its many faiths. Amen!

Responses

Michael Fitzgerald

Bishop Fitzgerald argued that, rather than trying to *overcome* all the significant differences between their two faiths, Christians and Muslims should in the first place seek to *understand* those differences in a spirit of mutual acceptance of one another as people fundamentally oriented towards God. This should not be a purely static process; Dr Cerić's idea of 'designing value together' is echoed, for example, in Vatican documents which speak of the need to 'walk together toward truth and to work together in projects of common concern'.[15] Such an attitude in turn implies that truth is not to be seen as an object in the possession of one particular group; indeed, for Christians truth is best understood as a Person by whom they are themselves possessed. This involves a process of continuing revision of preconceived ideas, a journey of walking towards a goal which invites rather than imposes itself. It is this vision which lies behind the Second Vatican Council's insistence on the importance of religious liberty for individuals and communities:

> Truth can impose itself on the mind of man only in virtue of its own truth, which wins over the mind with both gentleness and power.[16]

Safeguarding religious liberty implies a respect for the place of religious identity within society. The challenge here is to build up what Dr Jonathan Sacks, Chief Rabbi of the United Hebrew Congregations of the Commonwealth, has described as a 'community of communities', where diverse religious identities can be lived out in open communication. This is a task that requires religious groups and their leaders to develop a 'double language', to be able both to speak in the terms of their own tradition and also to share in a wider discourse within society. It is against a nuanced background such as this that the question of the cultural and spiritual roots of Europe in particular needs to be addressed. Christianity has played a decisive role as a foundation of European culture, yet the historical part played by other sources, and the contemporary presence of a variety of other religious communities, must also be taken into account. Christians and Muslims may be helped to be more open to one another through recognizing and participating in this wider diversity.

Religions and cultures

Questions of religion in relation to culture are complex, being viewed differently in different parts of the Christian and Muslim worlds, and indeed by different people in the same place and of the same faith. For example, situations where there is a generally assumed intersection of religion and culture can be problematic for those who convert to either Islam or Christianity from another background. Indeed, from the latter perspective theology can be seen as a unifying factor in a faith community precisely in so far as it is distinct from, and transcendent of, cultural differences.

In many contexts, however, cultural, religious and political alignments are superimposed on one another in such a way that people's faith can easily be exploited or subverted for other ends. For minority communities in particular – whether Muslims in Western Europe or Christians in Pakistan, for example – this can lead to pressure to choose between the equally unpalatable alternatives of assimilation and isolation described in Dr Cerić's paper. There is pain from all communities which needs to be heard and acknowledged here, yet the hinterland of meaning, hope and identity which both Christians and Muslims find in God can empower them to cooperate in facing the shared challenges of living out their faith in the cultures within which they are set.

Similarities and differences

What importance should Muslims and Christians assign respectively to the similarities that they find between their faiths and to the differences which also exist? A variety of answers can be found to this question. Dr Cerić suggests that, paradoxically, it is the similarities, rather than the differences, that can make Muslims and Christians feel that they are so far from each other; it would in some ways be easier for each to talk to adherents of a radically different tradition such as Buddhism. On the other hand, some feel that the differences between these two monotheistic faiths are relatively insignificant when set against the challenge of secularism which confronts them both: a common witness to the transcendent presence of the divine is the message with which both Christians and Muslims have been entrusted for the world's sake. Yet may there not also be real, perhaps irreducible, differences even in this controlling vision of God – and may not the true test of the dialogue's maturity lie in facing those differences honestly and creatively? One practical step which could help careful analysis of these issues might be a scholarly project to draw up a comparative concordance of key theological and ethical concepts in the Jewish, Christian and Islamic scriptures.

Besides the issues of similarity and difference between Christianity and Islam, almost equally important is the recognition of the huge diversity within each faith. Christians and Muslims in different parts of the world use different languages and thought forms to interpret their beliefs and experiences, and sometimes the mutual transparency between, say, a Christian and a Muslim in an Arabic context may seem greater than that between two Christians in totally different cultural worlds. Each faith in each place, besides this, includes a wide range of attitudes and approaches to the contemporary world. Perhaps Muslims in recent years have suffered most from being misrepresented as a simply 'monolithic bloc', with the further consequence that some of the more marginal voices among them have been taken to be speaking for the whole Islamic community. Diversity and genuine pluralism within both Christian and Muslim traditions needs to be recognized equally by co-religionists and by members of the other faith.

Magnificat – Allāhu akbar

Kenneth Cragg

Divine power and human meaning

Magnificat and *Allāhu akbar* are the sure doxologies with which our two faiths begin, however in part divergent our entire theologies. They serve well to set thought on its way in relation to doctrine. There needs to be throughout a strong desire for realism, for what Muhammad Arkoun has called 'mental space' in which we reach beyond what he names 'false tolerance' and come to genuine meeting of minds concerting – and concerning – the whole range of our convictions.[17] For there is much that is elitist about dialogue, and remote from the passions in the street. Courtesy needs to dwell deep, lest what is only sanguine in meeting foregoes its full meaning.

Magnificat is where we can begin in praise of *al-asmā' al-husnā*, 'the divine Names'.[18] Praise and theology are properly one. We conceptualize God in thought: we acknowledge Allah in our worship. In either, in each, we aim to fulfil the rubric *kabbirhu takbīran*,[19] which uses what grammarians call an 'absolute accusative' to intensify the sense and its urgency: 'Make him greatly great.' Does this hint that there may be disparities in the discerning quality of the praise we bring? How do we 'make Allah great'? There is a vast difference between magnitude and magnanimity. What have we all intended when we have said, so often, 'I believe in God Almighty'? In what does Almightiness consist? In terms of what is *Allah al-qādir 'alā kulli shay* – 'omnipotent over all things'? The Islamic accent has often been on total and unquestioned power to will and ordain and determine the human scene, and Christian thought too has sometimes had a similar view. At all costs we need to align that divine dominance loyally with the biblical and Qur'anic truth of creation and, over it in *khilāfa* (or 'dominion'), the human *khalīfa* deputizing for God in the given dignity of 'vice-regent' holding a divinely given but essentially human 'subsidiarity' as set over nature under God. It is clear, in our common doctrine of creation, that a real entrustment has been placed in our care. All our agriculture, all our technology, is divinely entrusted to our human hands. (In the heavenly council, this *amāna* is decreed and affirmed as the divine will even against the demur and apprehension of the angels about its wisdom.)[20]

This situation in no way jeopardizes the sovereignty of Allah: it clearly conditions it partially on the due obedience, or *islām*, of us humans, so that – in measure – as concerns culture and civilization the will of Allah is done only as we make it our own, which of course is the whole thrust of prophethood: to teach, inform, enlist and direct that very *islām*, the due and freely brought human cognizance of the divine patterns our surrender to their norms of our own will must bring. Such acceptance to be and to serve 'on behalf of God' in the world is plainly volitional and in no way automatic. There would be no point in sending prophets to puppets.

The point might be intriguingly made by asking – oddly – why *Allāhu akbar* needs to be said. Does it not 'go without saying'? – God, divinely great being indubitable, altogether true. Yet Magnificats need to be uttered. The God who is has 'to let be'. Indeed, 'letting God be' is the whole thrust of Islam, the entire disavowal of all the *shirk* that disallows the sense of him – in the sense of Surah 17.111, we have 'to make Him great'.

In what, however, do we see the 'greatness' to consist? Our answering theology must be consistent – as a doctrine of omnipotence – with the meaning of creation and responsible creaturehood where the world is given into trust and human liability. Muslims and Christians need to see and confess their community in this vision of vocation inside the natural order and escape the mutual enmity that so long prevailed in history. It is all there in the question of Surah 7.172: *a-lastu bi-rabbikum*, 'Am I not your Lord?' The passage has to do with a cosmic pledge (answering it) drawn from all humanity in the womb of the future to the end of time. It is pre-Noachide, pre-Sinaitic covenanting that 'binds over' all humans to the recognition of God. For all have answered: 'Yes, we so witness . . .'. No generation can consider itself exempt from the summons Godward, nor can any blame their forebears for misleading them.

Note that the vital question is in the negative – the sort that expects the Yes answer, but waits for it. It does not impose: it awaits consent – and this is 'God Almighty speaking'. It needs to echo through our mosques and churches, because our human meaning turns on the divine question, and the divine question entrusts us with the answer. All hinges on Surah 2.30 as a kind of meta-narrative teaching how we should understand our being here on this benign planet, caring in God's name for the good earth on God's behalf.

This biblical/Qur'anic reading of creation-under-human-care is not answering the question 'How?' in a crude creationism. (Evolution may, in measure, say 'how'.) It is the perception of all things as divinely 'let be', divinely wanted, having behind them a loving *niyya*, or intention,[21] so that life and the world do not constitute a fraud or a delusion: they tell a 'meantness' in which we humans are called to share in gratitude and wonder and resolve, by what has been called the anthropic principle[22] being generously present in our creaturehood. This meaning of Surah 2.30 (and cognate passages) is a deep philosophy of history. The Lord bids the angels 'worship Adam', in recognition of the divine stake in the human order. All but Iblis (*al-Shaitān*) reluctantly do so, Allah having dismissed their fears that the human creature is too fickle, too bloodthirsty, to fill the high dignity. The Lord is resolved on the risk involved.

Satan determines to entrap and beguile the creature he despises so that he can show Allah the folly in creation. In turn, we have to give the lie to this 'accuser' of our meaning and so in turn vindicate the Lord. Satan's 'Has God said?', his suspicions to us that our autonomy is unreal, or that we should repudiate the dignity of any *islām* with it – all these conspiracies of sin have to be resisted or overcome. That supreme goal and purpose is the business of religion. Hence Islamic *huda* ('guidance'), *dhikr* ('reminder'), *dīn* and *taqwā* ('piety') and all the 'messengers' of counsel, warning and tuition.

We can quickly see how relevant, how 'existential' this *mise-en-scène* is, and how vital to the role of true religion in civilization and culture and the economic order on which they rest. There is so much in modern life that does not want to 'be scripted' in this way, as playing a role of which the text has been prescribed elsewhere (in our case, 'from heaven'). People want a 'sovereign self' free 'to do their own thing', yet more and more finding that culture subjugates and imprisons them. Hence the malaise, the addictions, the aimlessness, the despair of ever being 'genuine' in selfhood in what we may call 'modernity'. Hence, in turn, the unlovely absolutisms into which some religion descends, as if that vital 'Yes' to 'Am I not your Lord?' was never asked of us and was never in our free power to give.

The sacred and the secular

Here our theology has to allow – in this limited sense – the actuality of the 'secular'. The option is there: what Surah 7.172 holds is not an imposition but an invitation. The 'secular' – the whole order of life as the realm of decision – is the raw material of the 'sacred', just as the 'sacred' is the destiny of the 'secular'. To be sure, as Islam loves to insist, 'Everything is tributary to Allah; nothing is outside his sovereignty'. That remains eternally true so long as we do not assume that it happens without us – happens, that is, in those reaches of our autonomy that are genuinely given into our trust.

If all things were somehow mechanically 'hallowed', not always inside the crisis of our *taqwā*, it would not be our sort of world, nor would it tally with the creaturehood our scriptures tell us is ours. Everything 'secular' – our creaturely powers, our sexuality, our trading and managing and discovering and harnessing – are awaiting 'consecration' at our hands and the crisis is perennial, perpetual. But the destiny of all to be brought within that seeking, querying, patiently waiting, divine intention for them forbids that they should ever be 'secular' in any final sense.[23] It is here that our concept of 'Almightiness' is ripe for revision if we invoke it as if it had granted us no creaturely mandate. Such a false view there would be a great irony, in that the generosity so evident in creation is the crucial dimension in the divine 'greatness' itself. For *takbīr* was ours to render.

This common fact of our theologies is ever more important now, given the modern ('postmodern'?) mood of 'not believing in belief' and the incredible advances of technology – medical, chemical, military and commercial. For these have brought our creaturely autonomy into uncharted waters and into the menace of deceptive self-sufficiency. We cannot disinvent, but can we safely handle? Have our powers disenthroned our religions? Technologies are all within the given creaturely autonomy, but have they run away with the tether of faith?[24]

When our scientific techniques seem to be so competent, there is for many a recession in the sense of God or the place of prayer. The methodologies of science (for right internal reasons) make the laboratory (for example) a very circumscribed place. It focuses and concentrates, leaves out perspectives not immediately relevant. It tends to the view notably expressed by the novelist Iris Murdoch:

> That human life has no external point or *telos* is a view as difficult to argue as its opposite and I shall simply assert it. I can see no evidence to suggest that human life is not something self-contained . . . Our destiny can be examined but it cannot be justified or totally explained. We are simply here . . . a human experience has nothing outside it.[25]

That is quite categorical and it is where many people now are in both hemispheres. Thus it is a dire part of our 'inter faith' dialogue that we should reach into its agnostic confidence or its sceptical despair. Dialogue cannot be limited to a converse of theists.

For us human life is 'justified' as a magnanimous venturing of a divine compassion creating an arena wherein to be partnered by us humans, 'making the Author of the enterprise greatly great' by the praise wrought by our acceptance of it. The autonomy with which we are endowed to do so is the crux of our meaning as being 'over things' that we might thereby be 'under God'. Our theology of divine omnipotence has to be known in the mystery of our creaturehood under the aegis of prophethood – all of whose ministries of guidance, reminder, tuition and warning are reciprocal to our vocation. 'Am I not your Lord?'

This sense of things is in accord with the biblical/Qur'anic theme of the creature, Adam, being made conversant with the names of things. For 'naming', nomenclature, taxonomy, has always been basic to science. We identify and classify and so attain our competence. Nature, it has been said, makes no statements: it does answer questions. It is by interrogation, research, that we ascertain, in ever accumulating fullness. The whole proceeding attests the sort of divine magnanimity under which we live and act and wonder and attain. Our liberties are a clue to Allah's omnipotence – its measure and its patience.

It is worth remembering how human sexuality keeps the eternal creation alive. Procreation is a large theme in the Qur'an as a key to creation as a human trust.[26] In the mystery of parenthood, the total dependence of infancy, we sense the divine 'over to you' about all our experience as a destiny into 'charge', 'duty', 'trust' and 'vocation' in all the reaches of our culture and our story and thus, in all, to confess the Almighty Lordship that willed to have it so.

Authority as commendation

Surely one corollary of this sense of 'God Almighty' must be for all our 'clerisy' – sheikhs, pastors, mullahs and ministers – a corresponding grace in our custodianship of doctrines in God's name. Faiths need to be 'commended' in terms that suit their own quality as vested in the understanding of God. Paul says that 'God commends his love . . .'. [27] His Greek verb *sunistēsin* is almost 'Let us establish together', seeking and inviting – from the other party – a reciprocal recognition, so that each can truly say: 'I am persuaded . . . .' In that way, there would truly be 'no compulsion in religion', in line with the famous dictum (often over-ridden) of Surah 2.256.

Our 'official' custody of faith needs to seek the sort of reception that recognizes how Allah's own question is phrased. Dogmatic credentials should bring the kind of authority that elicits only what can answer with the integrity of sincere conviction. Too often what some have called a *magisterium* – whether of doctrine or of law – has ill-served the greatness of God, a greatness not made 'greatly great'[28] by the arrogance of its custodians. Religious authority, whether of institutional theology or of *velayāt-e-fuqahā*, needs to reach into and work with that 'witness on our souls' of which Surah 7.172 tells, never developing into a kind of tyranny over those 'souls' whom Allah has endowed with liable creaturehood. Perhaps one goal of our meeting should be a gentler, humbler discharge of all 'official' spirituality.

Can it be that the universal endowment of *khilāfa* and *amāna* ('the trust of the heavens and the earth' which humankind 'accepted')[29] embraces, in some measure, the 'lay' scrutiny of the credentials of faith? To be sure, not all can be experts or 'pundits'[30] but all must will to hold faith with all the integrity that illiteracy, poverty or other circumstances will allow. These privations should always be in our 'learned' sights. Thus the mutual doctrine of liable creaturehood requires a genuine 'laicization' of religious perception,[31] so that there is a place, too, for conscience in the reading of scriptures and the interpretation of Sharī'a. The question 'Am I not your Lord?' needs to reverberate through the corridors of religious institutions of thought, liturgy and jurisprudence. Religious leaders are no substitute for God.

These thoughts have a brevity that deserves better of their theme and its wider implications, but they inevitably lead into the large issue of other sorts of power than those that belong with theology and its organs and offices.

Religion and political power

The role of power and statehood bears vitally on the stance and the temper of religious faith-custody as inherently 'witness' and 'response' in terms of the inclusive divine question of Surah 7.172 and the cosmic human pledgedness to the reality of Allah, as both the set of mind and the rule of God. What part should, does, political power have in right reading of our divine human-ness under God? Power should certainly – and vitally – be engaged with the task of witness and truth-bearing that faith has, but not monopolistically as if faith had no independent and ever-critical role beyond and above such political means. We can never well identify the greatness of God, as vested in the human privilege, with the political order.

When the Convention People's Party worked in the late fifties of the twentieth century towards independence in Ghana, its leader Kwame Nkrumah adapted for a slogan the Sermon on the Mount, to read: 'Seek ye first the political kingdom and all other things will be added unto you.'[32] There was something of the same confidence in the *hijra* of the Prophet from Mecca to Medina, as a quest for the ultimate sanction of political power. In the former city, he had been repeatedly enjoined to understand that 'his sole responsibility was to bring the *balāgh*' (the message as witness, no more, no less).[33] He had been told: 'I (Allah) have not made you responsible for these people.'[34] He had been asked: 'Do you think you can compel men to believe?'[35] Islam holds strongly that the *hijra* into a power-complex in Medina in no way compromised those Meccan prescripts, rather that it was rightly drawn as a valid 'policy-for-polity' from the hostile refusal of the Quraish in Mecca to heed the patient *balāgh* of thirteen harsh years during which Muhammad was 'altogether distressed in soul by the way they were'.[36]

Islamic confidence in the rightness of political power in the defence and propagation of religion has persisted ever since and it remains a large issue in our inter-religious dialogue. To equate *dīn* with *dawla*, to identify citizenship with believing, to have Caliphate on behalf of Allah, to entrust orthodoxy to power – these have been fascinating in some measure to all religions. But does it not oversimplify the whole business of religion in the world and tangle religious integrity in these political auspices? If the faith is unilaterally one with the state, can faith retain the necessary accusation without which power drifts into quite irreligious self-corruption, as the way of power is?

21

It is intriguing that there is no mention of Caliphates political in the Qur'an and that the scripture itself provides very little of the actual Sharī'a in realms outside personal status law.[37] Ultimately there is no doubting the complete priority of Mecca in the ethos of Islam. It was the Meccan faith for whose sake the *hijra* into the Medinan dimension was undertaken in the first place. What followed, in no way mere adventurism into brigandage, was a purposeful campaign for a religion's sake. It is to Mecca that the *hajj* goes, on Meccan *qibla* that every mosque everywhere meticulously aligns itself. It is only as *rasūl* of God that Muhammad is credally designated, and the *rasūl* has only *risāla*, i.e. *balāgh* or 'message' in 'apostolate'. It must remain an urgent open question whether 'apostolate' for God can be wholly beholden to political order in that *cuius regio eius religio* long congenial to medieval Christendom and enduring into modern times.[38] However, Christianity always has for its final mentor those three founding centuries of New Testament and post-New Testament existence in powerlessness and much-persecuted reliance on 'witness' – on *religio per se*. In that respect, one may say that Muhammad in the Medinan *hijra* was his own 'Constantine'.

The issue stays. What is suggested by some Muslims is that what was right then, in the setting of seventh-century Arabia, is no longer right now, in the global scene and a twenty-first century. The quest for international law, human rights, legitimate feminism and other factors argue that, while religion must ever monitor power, it may not well exercise it in those inherently compulsive terms that power by nature assumes – terms that brook no welcome tolerance of diversity.

There are two practical present-day factors that bear on this 'separation' of faith from unilateral power-wielding. One is the diaspora of 'exilic' Islam; the other is the composite nature of many countries – like Nigeria, Uganda, Egypt, the Philippines, Lebanon and the rest – where common citizenship would be gravely threatened by exclusive religious control of power.[39]

In diaspora, Muslims – in all likelihood permanently – have only a Meccan situation, in that (apart from those who remain subversive in their havens)[40] they have their Islam as 'just a religion'. This is Mecca, pre-*hijra* but without the persecution. Mosques are open, *salāt* is made, pilgrimage avails, Ramadan is kept, *zakāt* is paid – what lacks of Islam? Is not their vocation as Muslims thus abidingly fulfilled even though they forego the comforting umbrella of exclusively Islamic statehood? May it not even be a more ultimate, as well as a more timely, Islamicity?

All must finally turn on how we reckon with 'the greatness of God'. For Christianity, in its defining origins, it was a greatness utterly generous in its creative magnanimity and even more so in stooping to 'our low estate' in the self-imaging so greatly given in the incarnate and redemptive Messiah Jesus, as the 'Word made flesh'. Islam 'makes him greatly great' in the benediction of our human guiding into rightness by the textuality of sacred *tanzīl* and the summons into obedience by the discipline and the nurture ordained for us in the Qur'an and the Sharī'a.

Two faiths are one in the mystery of our created human trust of human privilege in the world of our mortal regime on his behalf. For us each it is a divine 'greatness' great enough to delegate, great enough to risk the risk we constitute. As for how that 'risk' proceeds in the scenarios of history we are – in part – at odds about 'education' or 'redemption', and, in consequence, about how political power belongs with our entrusted truth. Brevity means despair about being adequate, so that 'to finish is never to conclude' – which in such a place as this is how it should be. We might end with John Donne's warning (reading in 'power' both systems of doctrine and realms of politics):

> That thou mayest rightly obey power, her bounds know;
> Those past, her nature, and name is chang'd; to be
> Then humble to her is idolatrie.[41]

And, over all, do we not need the prayer of the poet Gerard Manley Hopkins?

> Make mercy in all of us, out of us all mastery,
> But be adored, be adored King.[42]

Response

Sohail Nakhooda

Mr Nakhooda outlined some of the difficulties that he as a Muslim found in Bishop Cragg's approach. This seems to be a very Christian, and to some extent a sentimental, interpretation of Islam, and as such it exercises a certain amount of exegetical violence on the texts. Precisely because God is *akbar*, it is not possible to impose our categories on him. In particular, the balance between the various divine attributes needs to be respected, without undue prioritization of the categories of forbearance and grace. In terms of witness to divine activity also, a passive approach is not sufficient. Like the Qur'an, the Old Testament recognizes that God uses whatever is best to fulfil his purposes – as emphasized, for example, in the centrality of the Exodus in liberation theology.

This means in turn that 'the secular' can have no real integrity for Muslims. God is to be worshipped in every place, and the 'entrusted-ness' which he gives to us should not be construed from a negative starting-point. Islam is not an act of compromise; on the contrary, awareness of our radical finitude means that we cannot become too adapted to this world.

Human autonomy and accountability

Bishop Cragg's presentation and Mr Nakhooda's response clearly take very different positions with regard to the question of human autonomy in relation to God. Some Muslims, though, would want to probe the middle ground between them. If Islam assumes some measure of human autonomy, what are the limits of that autonomy? Might we say that in some sense secularity itself also needs the direction that faith supplies? On the other hand, for Christians – particularly in the Western world – the issue rather is, given the way in which human *autonomy* has developed in the direction of self-sufficiency, how the theme of human accountability can be reinstated. In the first place, this is an *accountability* before God, but in both faiths that extends also to an ethical responsibility towards fellow humans and towards creation itself.

If Christians and Muslims are wrestling in their communities with these twin issues of accountability and *autonomy* respectively, is it possible that together they can learn from one another what it means to live responsibly before God in the complexities of the contemporary world? Through such shared learning, can they together become a sign of blessing for all God's creation?

Chapter 2
Learning from history

In order to understand where Christians and Muslims are in their present relations, we need some awareness of the ways in which the two traditions have interacted with one another in the past. Yet this is no straightforward matter, for there is no one simple Christian–Muslim 'history'. Rather, there is a complex pattern of interlocking relationships and failures of relationships, strikingly different in different periods and places, and moreover often perceived in radically different ways by Muslims and Christians sharing the same periods and places. In such a situation, it is difficult to speak of 'learning from history' in any univocal way; yet historical research still has great relevance for present-day realities. Negatively, it provides an invaluable corrective to over-simplified generalizations, which can easily distort contemporary understandings of the 'other' in either community. Positively, while the past cannot be altered, the way in which it is remembered is not beyond our control. By their choice of key episodes on which to focus, and by their interpretations of those episodes, historians can significantly influence perceptions and attitudes in the present, and so help to shape the future.

These considerations are recognized, and their implications demonstrated, in the two papers in this chapter, which give respectively a Christian and a Muslim reflection on some salient points of the Christian–Muslim past. **Professor David Kerr** points out the inadequacy of the traditional model of two separate circles, representing 'the (Christian) West' and '(Eastern) Islam'. The diverse interactions of Christians and Muslims across the globe and through history are better conceptualized within the one embracing circle of the whole human community. **Professor Tarif Khalidi** highlights changing perceptions of Christians from the viewpoint of Muslims through four periods, and draws together some of the persistent themes evident in the interaction of the two faiths. Building on careful approaches to history of this kind enables a fresh and critical appraisal of some of the rhetoric which dominates contemporary discussion of Christian–Muslim relations. At the same time, the contemporary significance of much of the historical inheritance remains contested. For example, the meaning of the *dhimma* (system of 'protected minorities' in traditional Islamic societies) continues to generate forceful debate between and among Christians and Muslims today.

Christian–Muslim relations: lessons from history

David Kerr

Introductory clarifications

Let me begin with some qualifications to the title I have been given: 'Christian–Muslim relations: lessons from history'. Firstly, I shall emphasize the initial part of the hyphenation, and focus on the Christian dimensions of relationship with Islam. To speak fully of 'relations' is to include issues of mutuality and reciprocity. It is not my intention, however, to discuss Muslim views of, or relations with, Christianity. Muslim scholars will do this themselves, and their insights would make redundant anything I could offer.

Secondly, it is hazardous to draw 'lessons from history'. The history of Christian relationships with Islam does not present itself as an objective record from which principles can be abstracted, universalized and applied to our contemporary situation. On the contrary, any historical review of Christian perspectives on Islam will show that these are inherently contextual in nature, defined by the particularities of time, place and culture. I start, therefore, from the axiom that historiography is subjective in being largely determined by the *a priori* assumptions of the historian, and reflects that person's perspectives and starting points.

Thirdly, I am not so much a historian as one interested in religious ideas, and their power to influence, while at the same time being influenced by, the way people act. So, rather than attempting a detailed history of Christian–Muslim relations, I propose to select moments from that history that, to my mind at least, reflect significant intellectual perspectives of Christian reflection on Islam.

Finally, we need to think about the present and future challenges of Christian–Muslim relations. While dealing in some sense with history, this paper will also try to imagine the future. Christian theology is eschatological: its concern lies with the ultimate fulfilment of God's purposes as these are revealed in history, and discerned in the continuing human struggle for faithfulness expressed in lives and communities of justice and peace.

I see this, equally, as the ultimate and urgent responsibility of Christian–Muslim relations. Religion has resumed a new priority with the postmodern collapse of confidence in secular or other ideological visions of human society. It is imperative, therefore, that faith addresses the public sphere, and my interpretation of Christian relationships with Islam will attempt to do so.

Starting points?

More than a quarter of a century ago the late Professor Wilfred Cantwell Smith raised the question of starting points: how to begin to conceive the relationship between Christianity and Islam. The traditional approach has been to visualize the two religions, and the civilizations they have helped to create, as separate circles: their circumferences may touch, but they remain discrete and encounter each other, face to face. Confrontation becomes the operative metaphor, and history is constructed in terms of a potential or actual 'clash of civilizations'.

Much scholarly literature on Christian–Muslim relations demonstrates that this is the dominant line of approach, which is precisely what Professor Smith wished to challenge. 'A different – and I would submit, a truer – perception and formulation of that history', he wrote, 'will be the work of someone who sees himself or herself as within the total complex, and can present it therefore so.'[1]

Professor Smith's call for a new mental map of Christian–Muslim relations is the more urgent today in light of the changing demography of Christian–Muslim encounter. The classical two-circle vision was premised on Christendom's identification with Europe, confronting an Islamic world that began in Western Asia and North Africa. The twenty-first century presents us with different realities. A majority of Christians now live in the Southern and Eastern hemispheres, outnumbering Western Christians by a ratio of three to two. It is no longer possible, therefore, to equate Christianity simply with Western culture and history. In the phrase of the West African theologian, Kwame Bediako, Christianity is 'renewing itself as a non-Western religion'.[2] As part of this rediscovery, Christians in many parts of Africa and Asia are living in societies in which Islam is an important socio-cultural ingredient. Western Christian perspectives on Islam are increasingly irrelevant to such situations, and non-Western Christians are searching for contextually valid approaches to inter-religious relationships.

The complementary reality is that twentieth-century Islam has seen significant growth in the West, in Australasia as significantly as in Europe and North America. Addressing the situation in the United States, Ibrahim Abu Rabi' argues that Muslims are 'paving the way for the formation of a universal Islamic culture – with unique American characteristics – within the boundaries of secularism'.[3] Islam, by this reckoning, can be authentically Islamic while at the same time being authentically American, and we are challenged once again to reshape our mental cartography of the conditions under which Islam and Christianity encounter within the West.

With respect to Professor Smith however, his question arose less from the changing religious geography than from the subject matter of religion itself. The dominant model of Christian–Muslim encounter examines the external manifestation of religion: most Christian perceptions of Islam have privileged the language of belief (*lex credendi*), its institutional expressions, and socio-political ramifications – evidence, contemporary fascination with so-called Islamic 'fundamentalism'. But several twentieth-century scholars have called for a perspective that engages the inner life of Islam and Islamic society. Constance Padwick's *lex orandi*, Louis Massignon's *commercium in spiritualibus*, Kenneth Cragg's 'call to retrieval' each challenge Christians to engage the interiority of Islamic concern, exemplifying what the Vatican calls the 'dialogue of the spirit'.

I do not present these as alternative starting points, or suggest that they are exclusive of each other. Rather, a comprehensive approach to Christian–Muslim relations needs to balance them all, in order to offset the mono-dimensional and anachronistic view of Islam that prevails in much of the public discourse of Western Christian and post-Christian society.

Seventh-century beginnings

The redrawing of our mental map of Christian–Muslim relations can be facilitated by identifying new myths – in the Greek sense of *mythos* – to inspire the imagination. These must, of course, be rooted in history. An especially powerful one is found in that early moment in the history of the nascent Muslim community, while it was still based in Mecca, when the Prophet ordered the first converts to seek refuge in the court of the Christian *Negus* of Abyssinia: there, to quote words attributed to the Prophet, was 'a king who rules without injustice, a land of truthfulness'. Granted, this was intended only as an interim measure, 'until God leads us [i.e. the Muslims] to a way out of our difficulty'.[4] Yet it was the context in which Muslim exegetes of the Qur'an interpreted the reference in Surah *al-Mā'ida* to the Christians being 'closest in love to those who believe'.[5]

This early evidence of Muslims and Christians sharing common social and spiritual space reminds us that the history of Christian–Muslim relations began not as two separate circles confronting each other, but was so – if the circle metaphor is appropriate at all – in their eclipse. This may not be the best choice of word either, for it was not a matter of one circle darkening the other. On the contrary, the mythic value of this incident is that each illuminated the other. It was, we are told, the Muslims' veneration of Mary (*Mariam*) that moved the *Negus* to draw a symbol in the sand to indicate the extent to which Christians and Muslims share a common faith.[6]

Arab Christianity and Islam

Myths are tested in their ability to shape imagination. In the development of the Caliphate under the Umayyad and Abbasid dynasties, Christians living within its domains began to image an interpretation of Christian faith that engaged Islamic realities. Early evidence of this can be seen in the theological writing of the Melkite monks of Mar Saba monastery, in the Cedron Valley east of Bethlehem. Originally a Greek *lavra*, Mar Saba was the place where Arabic replaced Greek as the language of Palestinian Christian theology, reflecting the linguistic shift from Greek to Arabic as the administrative language of the Umayyad Caliphate.

It was to Mar Saba that St John of Damascus (d. 749) retired from serving the Caliphate to write his theology. He did so in Greek, his familiarity with Arabic being a debated question. His successor, Theodore Abu Qurra (d. 820), wrote in both Greek and Arabic. By the mid–ninth century a first systematic explanation of Christian theology was written entirely in Arabic. Sydney Griffiths has observed that: 'The time was now ripe for a comprehensive presentation of the Christian point of view, taking into account the new socio-political realities of life under the rule of Muslims.'[7]

Further east, in Baghdad, where the Assyrian Patriarchate had moved from its original home in Celeusia Ctesiphon, the eighth- to ninth-century Patriarch Timothy debated with Caliph al-Mahdi, and affirmed that Muhammad 'walked in the path of the prophets'.[8] A diplomatic answer, perhaps, but one that can be accepted at face value.

It was this same patriarch who supported Assyrian (Nestorian) missions to Tang dynasty China where, on the evidence of the Nestorian tablet and other Christian manuscripts, the Assyrian Christians were willing to go a long way in contextualizing their Christian faith in other religious cultures and concepts. In the words of the contemporary Antiochian Orthodox bishop, Georges Khodr, they sought 'to nurture the spiritual tradition of religions [they] encountered by "improving" them from within, while not "alienating" them'.[9]

It would, of course, be naïve to ignore Eastern Christianity's historical capacity for anti-Islamic polemics. Equally, although persecution was mercifully rare, later Muslim society marginalized the participation of Eastern Christians, and a *dhimmī* culture was created in which Eastern Christians tended to turn in on themselves. The Orthodox historian, Robert Haddad, has noted that it was still possible, however, for Eastern Christians to make their influence felt in times of social and intellectual renaissance (*nahda*): in the flourishing of philosophy in tenth-century Baghdad, for example, or when the revolutionary nature of Arab nationalism was being explored in late nineteenth-century Syria and Egypt. Haddad concludes that, in social and cultural terms, Eastern Christians feel themselves more at home in Islamic than in Western society.

This expresses the mythic value of Eastern Christianity's engagement with Islam. It was not a question of two discrete circles touching one another, but of two religious traditions sharing a common cultural matrix to which each contributed.

Western Christianity and Islam

The context of early Christian–Muslim encounter in the West was very different, although almost as ancient as that of the East, originating with the Arab-Berber conquest of Spain in the early eighth century. A difference of perspective is immediately evident. Whereas many Eastern Christian historians saw the expansion of Islam as a liberation of Monophysite Christianity from the shackles of the Byzantine Empire, Latin historians viewed the conquest of Spain as an alien invasion: an alien and infidel people imposing their power over Christendom. The cry '*Moros en al costa*' (the Moors have landed) was to have an enormous mythic power over the minds of Christians in Portugal, Castile and Aragon until the end of the fifteenth century and beyond.

While historical evidence does not support an interpretation of popular antipathy toward the Saracen in terms of the later concept of race, many Spanish Christian writers condemned Islam culturally and religiously. The military character of the eighth-century Muslim conquests, and of the long-drawn wars of Christian *reconquista* that began in the eleventh century, account for the tendency of Spanish Christian writers to identify Islam with violence. The perceived moral laxity of the Cordoba Caliphate led Christians to complain that formerly Christian lands were now polluted by Muslim rule; and the need to redeem them provided the religious justification of the *reconquista*. A few Christian theologians went so far as to identify Islam with the apocalyptic vision of the beast in the Book of Daniel. As the Prophet Daniel was exiled in Babylon, Eulogius of Cordoba felt spiritually exiled in a Christian Spain under Muslim rule. It was an easy step for him to interpret Daniel's vision of the fourth beast with the Saracen kingdom: 'It shall devour the whole earth, tread it down, and crush it.'[10]

Eulogius' complaint evidences another reality, however: that of cultural interaction among the Christians and Muslims of Andalusia. Too many young Christians, he regretted, were forgetting Latin in an eagerness to converse in Arabic. Here we have ninth-century evidence of the emerging Mozarabic culture of Andalusian Christianity, a Christianity that in literary, liturgical and architectural terms styled itself on Arab cultural mores. Mozarabic Christianity in turn contributed to the wider *convivencia* that flourished in the twelfth and thirteenth centuries under the Berber dynasties of Spain. The Jewish philosopher Maimonides confessed in his *Guide for the Perplexed* that 'It was from the Arabs that our co-religionists borrowed whatever they borrowed, and it was their method that they followed'.[11] He was referring, of course, to the tradition of Arab-Islamic philosophy – al-Farabi, ibn Sina (Avicenna), and above all the great Spanish Muslim philosopher, ibn Rushd (Averroes). Christians made equal use of this same tradition: St Thomas Aquinas quoted Avicenna, to argue against Averroes, to make a point of Christian dogma in his *Summa Theologiae*. Amid the warfare of medieval Spain, Jewish, Christian and Muslim theologians found a common language in philosophy.

The most colourful, and perhaps the most complex, Christian character of this period was Ramon Lull, mystic, theologian, and missionary. His little *Book of the Gentile and the Three Wise Men*, written in Mallorca *circa* 1275, tells of a Gentile's search for true religion through conversation with three sages, a Jew, a Christian and a

Muslim. Each commends his religion with courtesy to the others, and without a hint of polemics. The Gentile finally holds his own counsel as to which of the religions he would choose. In the meantime – and this is the point of the story – the Jew, Christian and Muslim promise to continue their conversation until, 'agreed on one faith, they would go forth into the world, giving glory and praise to the name of our Lord God'.

Ramon Lull is a complex figure because he personified the two conflicting myths that arise from medieval Spain. On the one hand he was the personification of *convivencia*, his entire *Ars Magna* being an attempt to find a mystical reconciliation between Christianity and Islam, and one of his scholarly goals being to foster the study of Arabic in the European universities of his day. On the other hand, he supported the idea of the Crusade as the military strategy of 'taking the Cross' for the redemptive reconquest of Christian lands: Jerusalem and Andalusia. Medieval Christendom itself oscillated between these two poles, and though its dominant mode of encountering Islam centred around the latter, the former was never entirely abandoned.

Imperial Christianity and Islam

It is easy enough to identify when the Crusades began. Alphonso VI of Leon conquered Toledo in 1089, and Pope Urban II declared the First Crusade at the Council of Clermont in 1095. These, together with the Papacy's power struggle with the Holy Roman Emperor, reflect the political and ecclesiastical concerns that undergirded the Crusades. Compounded by the pressures of a rising population in Europe and the economic needs of land-owning classes, Jonathan Riley Smith interprets the Crusades as the beginning of the 'Expansion of Europe'.

Initially their main energy was directed to the East with the creation of the Latin principalities of Antioch and Edessa, and the Kingdom of Jerusalem. Defended with diminishing success over the next two centuries, the fall of Acre in 1291 marked the end of the Eastern Crusades. But this did not mark the end of the Crusades as a Christian strategy against Islam. The Crusading idea continued in Latin Christendom at least until the Reformation, and it was given renewed papal validation in the final struggle of the Catholic Monarchs of Castile and Aragon for the reconquest of the Emirate of Granada. As L. P. Harvey, historian of this last period of Islamic Spain, has shown, it was the success of the *reconquista* of Andalusia that led the kings of Portugal and Castile to give unqualified support to the *outre mer* expansion of their respective realms.[12]

In opening the Atlantic sea route to New Spain, Columbus was intent on finding a way to India that would circumvent the Islamic heartlands, while the Papacy was facing the expansion of the Turks towards central Europe. The mythic Prester John, the shadowy figurehead of a reputed Christian kingdom in the East – whether in Africa or Asia was a matter of dispute – held the promise of an anti-Islamic alliance on which a final Crusade could be mounted from both a Christian East and West. The dream evaporated, but Portuguese colonization in Africa, South and Southeast Asia carried the old crusading idea into new realms.

The historic legacy of the Spanish and Portuguese was Christendom's fixation on Islam as a geo-political problem, with the assumption that it had to be met by force. The Iberian drama of warfare between Christianity and Islam was exported and universalized as the dominant myth of Christian–Muslim relations. Mindanao Muslims were dubbed Moros by the Spanish, and the old battles were fought anew.

The alternative vision of *convivencia* would have been extinguished but for the solitary efforts of occasional Christian ecumenists and missionaries. Somewhat in the spirit of St Francis of Assisi, who accompanied the Fifth Crusade but sought to engage the Sultan of Egypt in spiritual discourse, the German Nicolas of Cusa envisioned a theological dialogue with the Turks, based on his Platonic conviction that 'there is one religion in a variety of rites' (*una religio in rituum varietate*). St Francis Xavier led his fellow Jesuits in Goa to establish an intellectual dialogue with Indian Muslim scholars in the Mogul court in Delhi. They applied the approach of St Thomas Aquinas in his *Summa contra Gentiles*: namely, to establish a philosophical common ground between Christianity and Islam as the prerequisite of interpreting the verities of Christian faith.

Europe's second era of imperialism, led by the Northern European powers from the eighteenth century, demonstrates continuities and discontinuities with the first. Believing in their mandate to civilize, colonial policies were rooted in European Enlightenment principles: the introduction of the nation state that separated religion from the public sphere and the development of a secular culture through new systems of education and law. Colonial administrators tended to regard the religious facets of Islam as symbols of a dying past. Cromer's famous remark that 'reformed Islam is Islam no more' expressed the European consensus that Islam would not survive the civilizational revolution of imperialism. New caricatures populated the European mind and found dramatic expression in, for example, Voltaire's *Mahomet*: Islam as medieval obscurantism, fanatical, resistant of modernity.

The religious element of encounter was left to the missionaries, who were generally viewed by political administrators as coat-tailers who were barely to be tolerated. The missionary purpose of conversion always threatened to disturb the peace since it was so strongly protested by Muslim leaders. Yet within this objective, there were a range of missionary approaches to Islam. As Karl Pfander (d. 1865) pursued what he deemed to be the contradictions of Christian and Islamic beliefs, Isabella Reid – also of the Anglican Church Missionary Society – took 'an almost childlike pleasure in Persian and Armenian women for their own sake, without constant need for theological qualification'.[13] This concern for the human face of Islam finds more reflective expression in the work of the later CMS missionary in Cairo, Constance Padwick (d. 1968), to whom I have already referred. Her *Muslim Devotions*[14] is a study of the prayer life of Muslims as evidenced in popular prayer: it is through the *lex orandi* of Muslims that the spiritual values of Islam are best discerned.

The myths that Christians inherit from colonialism are varied: Islam as pre-modern in contrast to Western modernity; Islam as the antithesis of Christianity, a religion of law contrasting the Gospel of grace; Muslims as people of estimable human qualities, whose inner spirituality is touched by the Spirit of God.

Non-Western Christians and Islam

The need for a post-colonial perspective on Christian–Muslim relations is an urgent imperative. The demographic shifts to which I have referred were already signalled in the late nineteenth century. The fascinating story of Sadrach Surapranata (1835–1924) evidences the ability of indigenous Javanese Christians to re-express their Christian faith contextually. Trained in both Islamic and Christian theology, Sadrach founded the Group of Free Christians (*Golongane Wong Kristen Kang Mardika*), comprising several thousand Javanese. It was the largest indigenous movement towards Christianity in any nineteenth-century Islamic society. Sadrach understood Jesus as 'an exemplary figure whose entire life consistently proved the truth and triumph of his Christian *ngelmu* [wisdom] through obedience to the law even unto death'.[15] The law he preached was the Sermon on the

Mount, and he referred to it as the *syariat* that leads to perfection. Sadrach's movement was eventually suppressed by the Dutch authorities, missionaries and political administrators acting in consort, but many Indonesians remember it as an early expression of the movement for national independence.

The struggle for independence from western colonialism has been the *leitmotif* of Christian–Muslim relations elsewhere, in the Middle East – one thinks of Lebanon, Iraq, and Egypt – and in Africa where Christian–Muslim solidarity played its part in the independence movements of Tanzania and Nigeria.

The challenge is to continue such cooperation after independence has been gained. A persuasive proposal has been given by the Pakistani Christian theologian, Charles Amjad-Ali, who is as critical of the post-1960s liberal Christian espousal of dialogue as he is of earlier Western Christian missions. Dialogue, he argues, is not a business of finding common ground in some transcending principles or beliefs: that would be to presume a *meta-logue*, a universal discourse that transcends local realities. On the contrary, he insists, true *dia-logue* occurs when Christians and Muslims come together, each with their respective *logos*, and engage the common challenges of the social contexts that they share, struggling through (*dia*) the real issues of life.

My most memorable experience of this was in the United States, with a group of African-American Muslims and Christians. Their district was awash with drugs and drug-related violence. Recognizing that these were killing their children, irrespective of religion, they formed an inter faith action group, confronted the dealers night by night for six months, and eventually cleared the streets. Theologically conservative as they were, they learned to pray together, to share the insights of each other's scriptures, and to make common cause for justice and peace.

Conclusion

This review of Christian–Muslim relations is necessarily impressionistic: it is selective in what it has discussed, and can be faulted for neglecting matters that might give a different picture. But in light of the terrain that has been covered, the following conclusions can be drawn:

1. There is no single history of Christian–Muslim relations, no meta-narrative that can be applied to all situations. History is contextual, and a global understanding of history requires an openness to

dialogue among different contexts, and a willingness to open contextual perspectives to the critical examination of partners in dialogue.

2. The European/Western history of Christian–Muslim relations is but one contextual experience. It is itself a varied experience, inspired by competing myths: the dominant notion of Christian–Muslim confrontation that focuses on external social aspects of Islam is counterpoised by the tradition of *convivencia* in which Christians have searched with Muslims, and Jews, for a common language of faith.

3. The European experience is also varied in socio-political terms. The tragic breakdown of Christian–Muslim relationships in Bosnia and Kosovo (the absence of which is the most serious lacuna of this paper) points to enormous failures of understanding between Western Europe and the Balkans.

4. The conclusion that I wish to emphasize, however, is that Western European understandings of Christian–Muslim relations can claim global dominance only as a result of imperialism. The case of Sadrach Surapranata suggests that it was the Dutch rather than the Javanese Christians who believed in this hegemony. In our post-colonial world it is imperative, as a contribution to world peace, that Western perspectives on Christian–Muslim relations open themselves to self-critical dialogue with non-Western experiences.

These, in the case of the Middle East, are both more ancient and socially integrated than they are in the West, and it behoves Western clergy and politicians to learn from the historic experience of Christians in the Middle East before presuming to advise on the future of their relationships with Islam.

In other parts of Asia and Africa the relationship between Christians and Muslims is more recent, but no less challenging of Western stereo-types. Muslim–Christian solidarity within families, such as is common among the Yoruba in West Africa for example, or in the struggle for nation building, represent reservoirs of human experience from which Western Christians have much to learn in dealing with challenges that increasingly confront our own societies.

The issue that has not been directly addressed in this paper is Christian–Muslim relations in the context of the contemporary political struggles that define many aspects of radical Islam. This is not an oversight, but an intended reservation, determined to resist current attempts to revise history in light of our post-September 11 concerns.

I would simply say that Amjad-Ali gives us the right lead: Christian participation in effective dialogue with Muslims entails learning to address the actual social and political problems that afflict Asian and African societies. If it is fair to explain radical Islam as a form of liberation theology, southern-hemisphere Christians can bring their own traditions of liberation to a dialogue from which, I suggest, the West has much to learn.

Finally, it is as people of faith that we meet. Professor Smith, with whom I started, carefully distinguished between faith and belief: the former denotes an affective relationship with God, while the latter represents ways in which the faith relationship is intellectualized and expressed in credal statements and institutional traditions. Faith, he insists, is something that Christians and Muslims share; it is the common ground of our being. Muslim and Christian beliefs differ, as do our institutional traditions. But Professor Smith pleads with us to recognize that these differences are secondary: that the 'cosmic' issue is faith, and that faith, as a divine gift, unites us in the grace of God.

Thus, with Professor Smith, I conclude that we should conceive Christian–Muslim relations not as a convergence of separate circles, but as a single circle: a shared human community of faith, differentiated by beliefs and institutional traditions, yet eschatologically united in the struggle (*jihād*) to discern and conform ourselves to the purposes of God in a divided world.

Response

Mona Siddiqui

Dr Siddiqui emphasized the dangers of simplifying the history of Muslim–Christian relations. The 'fallacy of like-mindedness', that people necessarily share a common goal with similar understandings of faith and religion, can lead to serious misunderstandings when internal diversity and tensions were forgotten.

Reactions to the events of September 11 2001 demonstrate the continuing power of religion as a force in society, and the continuing influence of myths and prejudices drawn from the past. On one hand, Islam and Muslims were once again associated by many with violence and an attack on freedom. On the other hand, many Muslims responded defensively to this image with cheap anti-Western and anti-Christian polemics.

Within such a polemicized context, it is necessary to ask hard questions about the place and the usefulness of dialogue. Can the exchange of ideas and thoughtful argument draw in those with influence in political, legal and educational systems, and so effect changes at the level of popular realities? Certainly this will not happen without real honesty on the part of all, and there is a pressing need to develop new patterns of dialogue which are no longer viewed with suspicion by Muslims as a belated legacy of colonial discourse.

Historical myths living today

In the contemporary world, it can sometimes seem that those who speak most forcibly about Christian–Muslim relations are those who know least about their history. Ill-informed rhetoric endangers both communities through exposing them to powerful but misleading generalizations which see history exclusively in conflictual terms. It has been argued, for example, that, since the eclipse of the Cold War, opinion formers in societies of both 'the West' and 'Islam' have sought to put the other into the position of the new 'enemy'.

One way for Muslims to deconstruct views like this is through the Islamic centre taking more seriously the experience of the Islamic periphery. Similarly, Western Christians need to acknowledge the significance of non-Western Christianity – a point made forcefully in Professor Kerr's paper. Europeans also need to learn other ways of reading history than seeing it always through the prism of monolithic nation-states.

At the same time, there are positive images from the past which can be revitalized to give inspiration and hope in the current situation. One of the most powerful of these is that of the medieval Spanish *convivencia* between Muslims, Christians and Jews within the framework of an Islamic society. In historical reality, its harmonious philosophy was only shared among elite groups, and its resonance in modern times owes much to its championing as an alternative to Franco's repressive and uniformitarian ideology. Nevertheless, it can be accepted as a positive mythological symbol to encourage those searching today for a shared language for the coexistence of Christians, Muslims and other people. Bosnia too, in much more recent times, knew a pattern of people of different faiths living together in a shared community; it was the imposition of compart-mentalized and divisive approaches to religious identity that undermined this coexistence.

The spiritual foundation for *convivencia* – as also for the honourable place traditionally accorded to religious minorities in other Islamic countries – was an attitude of hospitality and welcome on the part of the majority community. In the same way, underlying the Muslim presence in Britain is the principle of Christian hospitality. In the case of England this was made possible through a gradual process (predating Muslim settlement) of the progressive removal of civic disabilities from minority groups – in the first place, non-Anglican Christians. Nevertheless, despite the very different histories involved, there is an important sense in which Christians and Muslims in both East and West now share in a commonwealth of mutual hospitality.

Learning from Muslim history

Tarif Khalidi

What can history teach us?

I have grown less and less certain that history has any lessons to teach us – certainly not any lessons that ordinary common sense would not normally teach us in the course of a lifetime of quiet armchair observation of experience. History is far too fickle a teacher, far too ambiguous. But if it has, strictly speaking, no lessons, does it retain some practicable value, some guidelines perhaps, which can spice or otherwise decorate a dialogue? To tell us that this or that state of affairs need not be so? That history has not one but many conflicting narratives? That the ideology behind history is essentially dialectical and hence in one important sense liberal? That its true value is that it keeps the status of problems open rather than shut?

In 1962, the distinguished British medievalist Sir Richard Southern published a small gem of a book entitled *Western Views of Islam in the Middle Ages*. It was basically a series of lectures and the lecture format may have imposed a slightly rigid pattern on the final product. What the book does is to divide the history of Western Christian perceptions of Islam into periods: the Age of Ignorance, the Age of Inquiry, and so forth. Although this time division into ages may be a bit forced and may reflect what were at all times the views of a small minority of Western Christian thinkers, the insights of Southern, his crystal prose, and the invitation implied in that book to other historians to practise the same sort of activity: all these make the book a model of its kind, and a model in the best sense of the term, a paradigm that makes one think.

Possessing powers far inferior to those of Southern, I am nevertheless tempted by his model to try to do something similar, but from the eastern shores of the Mediterranean Sea. In other words, I am going to try briefly to see whether it is possible to draw a sketch of Islamic views of Christianity in the Middle Ages and beyond – nor am I particularly sensitive about using terms like 'Middle Ages' in an Islamic context, provided one defines one's time-span. My scheme will of course suffer from the same weaknesses of structure that I attributed to Southern's scheme. I will try to draw out a few implications at the end.

The Age of Triumph (from Qur'an to Jahiz, seventh to ninth centuries)

The most prominent Qur'anic slogan in this regard is the verse:

> It was He who sent His prophet with right guidance and the religion of truth to make it triumph over all other religions, even if the polytheists are set against this.[16]

This is a verse which regularly appears on earliest Islamic coins and inscriptions. It is a triumphalist statement, an affirmation that, in the evolution of religions, Islam has finally triumphed over its tribal cousins. The Qur'an proclaims a debating triumph, and early Islamic history is seen as confirmation of this on the field of battle. As the religion with the truth, its truth, its version of history, is victorious over all other versions. But the general tone, as is well known, is by no means hostile. Many Christians, we are told, are more honest than many believers – although one detects a distinct Qur'anic preference for monastic over church or ecclesiastical Christianity.

This period of triumphalism finds its culmination in the works of the great Jahiz (d. 868). In Jahiz, we now have a vindication of Islam, this time not just as a version of history, but also as culture. In Jahiz, it is Islamic culture which is demonstrably superior to Christian and Jewish culture. This is because, for Jahiz, Islam inherited, or perhaps co-opted, not only all previous divine revelations but all earlier cultures as well. Thus, where Christian culture is concerned, Jahiz argues that it was guilty of snuffing out Greek philosophy until Islam succeeded in rescuing and reviving wisdom from the decadence into which it had been plunged.

The Age of Curiosity (tenth to fourteenth centuries)

This is an age characterized by intense examination of Christian texts – primarily the Gospels – in an attempt to show how Christians misinterpreted these texts to arrive at erroneous doctrines like the Trinity and the Incarnation. Thus, a thinker like Abu Hatim al-Razi (tenth century) argues that the sonship of Christ is in reality a metaphor rendered dangerously literal by Christians, and hence that the Gospels give no support whatsoever to contemporaneous Christian theology. On the other hand, Islam is made to fit into the biblical scheme of history and is, for instance, identified as the fourth and final world kingdom predicted in the Book of Daniel. This is a period of great interest to historians of religious encounters because Muslim texts contain a vast amount of material on debates with Christian theologians and minute examinations of Gospel texts. Attributed to the great al-Ghazali (d. 1111) is a treatise which controverts the Christian views of Christ's divinity through close analysis of Gospel texts. The view is advanced by some Muslim theologians that it was St Paul who first derailed the original message of Jesus. For these thinkers, St Paul is the person primarily responsible for Christian waywardness. Stripped of its Pauline content, pristine Christianity is indeed a complementary message, one which naturally bears witness to the truth of Islam. In the view of these Muslim thinkers, Christianity is an errant, not a false, religion.

The Age of Indifference (fourteenth to seventeenth centuries)

A sense may be glimpsed of an age when Islam was, by and large, indifferent to Christianity, secure in its belief that there is no longer much to learn from either attacking it polemically or studying it intensively. The complacent comment of ibn Khaldun about the renaissance in Europe is perhaps typical of this Age: 'and it has reached us that the Arts and Sciences are once again finding a ready market in the academies of Europe. And God knows best about this.' It is as if ibn Khaldun is saying that God can effect miracles even among European Christians.

The Age of Bafflement (eighteenth to twentieth centuries)

Why has the Christian West prospered while the Muslim nations have declined? This is a question which recurs in much Muslim speculation of this age, from Tunis to India, and it was no doubt triggered by spectacular Muslim defeats. In fact several prominent books by nineteenth- and early twentieth-century Muslim reformers carry precisely this title, or something very close to it. The Muslim response to this question spreads out across a very wide spectrum of answers, all the way from 'we have abandoned the true path of Islam and must return to it' to 'the Christian West does after all have quite a lot to teach us today, as we once upon a time taught it'. It is quite clear from the totality of Muslim answers to this question that the lessons to be learnt from the Christian West are predominantly scientific and technical in nature.

The figure of Jesus

One immensely rich vein to explore, running throughout these ages, is the Muslim fascination with the figure of Jesus.[17] A very problematic figure in the Qur'an but one whose legacy is love and peace, Jesus in *Hadīth* and *Sira* is a kindred spirit of Muhammad (e.g. the story of Muhammad's cleansing of the Ka'ba, when he ordered all icons washed out except an icon of the Virgin and Child), and a constant presence in Muslim ascetic and ethical literature. At the height of the Crusades, he is there on the side of the Muslims – the message that 'Jesus is ours not yours' is perhaps best developed in the writings of the great twelfth-century Damascene historian and anti-Crusader polemicist ibn 'Asakir. Among the modernist Muslim poets, one thinks of the Palestinian Mahmud Darwish, the Sudanese Muhammad al-Fayturi, and above all the Iraqi Badr Shakir al-Sayyab: all these see in him an essential figure of crucifixion and resurrection, an archetypal figure who accompanies all journeys of suffering, all 'romantic' experience, all liberation struggles.

A few lessons

1. One must *advertise* both the antiquity and the immense variety of this record. This long Christian–Muslim relationship is nowhere nearly as well known as it ought to be: a historical archive with massive literary and artistic dimensions in poetry, prose and works of art. Over all, however, the image of Christianity is very mixed, a love-doubt relationship perhaps, with love and admiration for certain salient Christian virtues – such as mercy, humility and monastic devotions – but deep suspicion regarding such dogmas as the Trinity, the Crucifixion, the Incarnation and Mariolatry. In early Muslim tradition and history, the kindness shown to very early Muslims by the Christian ruler of Abyssinia, the prestige of the Byzantine empire, and the high social status achieved by local Christian doctors,

astronomers, philosophers and state secretaries all contributed to enhancing the image of Christians inside early Muslim societies.

2. The humanist tradition in Islam (philosophy, natural science, *adab*, theology, even Sufism) is that branch of the tree of Islam which took most interest in Christianity, or which was closest to it in the common pursuit of scientific knowledge. But even the Shari'a, as it developed towards non-Muslims in the age of Ghazali and beyond, contains a large body of law pertaining to relations with non-Muslims, much of it of unusual human rights interest to us today, and most of it unstudied.

3. Such a broad spectrum of perceptions meant that Christianity was seen under many lights. This should immediately put us on guard against theories such as that of the 'clash of civilizations'. This theory is a misapplication of metaphor on an epic scale, one of those glaring instances where language misleads and obfuscates reality, where misuse of metaphor can engender enormous mutual suspicion. Nations clash, armies clash, interests clash. But, as can be seen from even a fleeting examination of the historical record, the two civilizations can more appropriately be said to have embraced, examined or even danced around each other. This is indeed what civilizations normally do – it may be better to speak of the 'tango of civilizations' rather than of their clash.

4. *Theology vs. Law*. To derive true lessons from this encounter, one must make use of theological speculation. Unfortunately, Muslim theology has not been very exciting in the last hundred years or so. In the past, the debate with Christian theology greatly enriched Muslim theology. Today, Christian theology still has much to teach Muslim theologians. Some of its major modern schools, such as liberation theology, existentialist theology, dogmatic theology, even 'God is dead' theology, have enormous contemporary relevance to a moribund Muslim theology. The Law, despite the stalwart service it has performed on behalf of Islam, ought not to be the only spokesman of Islamic culture.

5. We must be on our guard against anyone who maintains that *the attitude* of Islam to Christianity (or indeed to anything else) is X, Y, or Z . Sentences which begin with the phrase 'Islam teaches A, B and C', or 'Islam's attitude to X, Y and Z is such and such' are utterly modern. The more traditional view has always been to lay out a diversity of opinion, this being considered more conducive to truth. No pre-twentieth-century Muslim scholar would ever dream of using a phrase like 'The position of Islam on this is that'. He would always say:

'Scholar A says this, scholar B says that and so on; and I, poor scholar that I am, and much in need of God's mercy, would venture to say that scholar A is nearer to the truth. But God Almighty knows best.' But perhaps worst of all are such phrases as 'the Muslim mind-set', 'the Muslim world-view', and so on all the way down to that horrific phrase, 'Muslim rage'. Islam, exactly like Christianity, addresses us in many voices. Anyone who speaks of it as if it has only one voice is interested in it more as an instrument of power than as a system of belief or truth.

6. Across time, Muslim societies have been far more pluralistic in com-position than Western European Christian societies, which began to become pluralist only in the last century or so. Within Islamic lands and for a millennium or more there existed sizeable communities of non-Muslims. The Islamic corpus of writings on relations with non-Muslims should be of considerable interest to modern theorists of pluralism, whether Christian or otherwise.

Where we go from here is not really a historian's question. As a teacher, I would simply say that the most useful thing one can do is to continue to point to the richness and variety of this particular historical encounter, and to hope that eventually this encounter will receive the attention it deserves. In the United Kingdom in particular, the school history curriculum should be a matter of concern to us. When history at times like these acquires particularly vivid modern relevance, this concern should be redoubled.

And, finally, there is Palestine, a sorrowful 'lesson of history' if ever there was one. Palestine has always been of immense historical concern to both Muslims and Christians throughout the world. For a millennium and a half, large swathes of its history were bathed with peaceful coexistence. Christian and Muslim communities interacted, worshipped together, joined hands across what is now a century and more of struggle for liberation, and left behind a Palestinian skyline of minarets and church towers to be seen in all their architectural glory in Jerusalem. Much blood was shed on its soil, but that soil itself also witnessed centuries of splendid coexistence. There is no reason why Christian–Muslim dialogue should not pursue, indeed demand, the return of harmony in Palestine. Unless the present brutalities of Israeli occupation exercised against Christians and Muslims are ended, Christian–Muslim relations as a whole will continue to carry, just beneath their surface, a tension or strain ('strain' as in disease) that will threaten at any moment to break violently on to their surface.

Response

Yvonne Haddad

Professor Haddad raised the problem of the different perspectives given to history when viewed from the point of view of the powerful and from the point of view of the victims. Relations between Christians and Muslims have indeed in many ways a rich and varied heritage, but there is the danger that this richness can be used to justify victimization. In some cases, resolution of conflict on the part of the powerful actually involves suppressing or ignoring histories. By contrast, those with mentalities of victimization do not forget their history. In fact, differently victimized groups can become trapped in contests over history to establish which has the more painful story. Such competitive victimization can easily be misused by political forces, but it is necessary to stand back and ask about the underlying burden of victimhood for which people are seeking redress.

Historical considerations like this need to be applied to contemporary realities. The gap between the amnesia of the powerful and the memory of the victimized was apparent in reactions to the September 11 attacks, and in the United States' difficulties in appreciating realities on the ground in the Middle East. A sense of competitive victimization can also distort the part played by the Christian–Jewish relationship within Christian–Muslim encounter, placing Palestinian and other Arab Christians particularly in a very difficult situation. Some Muslims indeed might see 'Christianity stripped of its Pauline content', in Professor Khalidi's phrase, as bearing witness to Islam, but equally some involved in Jewish–Christian dialogue call for the deconstruction of New Testament Christianity to accommodate the principle of one covenant only for God's people, deeming this necessary as a consequence of the centrality of the Holocaust. It seems, though, that if the contribution of Paul were to be excised there would be an end to the historic Christian faith.

A contested historical heritage: *dhimma*

Contemporary debates about the significance of the *dhimma* provide striking examples of the way in which important motifs in the history of Christian–Muslim relations continue to be contested today. Some Muslims point to the institution as evidence of the recognized place guaranteed to Christians and other religious minorities in societies ordered according to traditional Islamic lines. Sometimes, a contrast is drawn between this traditional toleration and the long-standing historic enforcement of religious uniformity within Western Christendom. Many Christians, by contrast, point to the various civic and religious disabilities involved in *dhimmī* status, and to the payment of the *jizya* tax as the price of guaranteed protection. Whatever its merits or demerits as a historic system, though, is the concept of *dhimma* still of any relevance to contemporary Christian–Muslim relations?

One interpretation would see *dhimma* primarily as a juristic arrangement, a contract between the state and individuals, rather than as an ascription of status.[18] On this view, like any contract, it is in principle revocable, and it has in fact been ended in modern Islamic states where it has been replaced by the idea of citizenship. This is broadly consonant with the approach of those who are seeking to integrate contemporary human rights thinking within an Islamic matrix of values.

On the other hand, *dhimma* is seen by others in more personal terms. From an Islamic perspective, it can be taken to mean the commitment of Muslims to protect the fundamental dignities and entitlements of their non-Muslim neighbours. The Muslims of Srebrenica, it might be said, would have been protected from genocide if there had been a lively Christian equivalent of 'dhimmītude' to which they could have appealed.

For many Christians in Muslim-majority societies, though, the *dhimmī* experience and status survives, even if only informally present within an official discourse of shared citizenship. For them, it implies a sense of being second-class citizens within their own country, a position of inferiority, and even an internalized mentality of quiescence and submission. Such concerns can take on added force for minorities in contexts where an active process of Islamization is underway or in prospect.

In one sense, these debates centre on the contemporary meaning and continuing relevance of this one specific motif from the history of Christian–Muslim relations. Yet it is clear also that the interpretative questions open out into broader issues of structuring the religious guidance of plural societies, of negotiating the relations between majority and minority communities, and of safeguarding religious freedom for individuals and groups. Such challenges have always and everywhere, in a wide variety of contexts, been centrally important themes in relations between the two faiths. A balanced and critically aware reading of the historical evidence can be of great value to Christians and Muslims struggling with these perennial challenges in today's world.

Chapter 3

Communities of faith

Both Islam and Christianity understand men and women to be called by God into a community of faith, and both stress that this community has a visible shape and a concrete presence within the world. But this immediately raises a question: What is the relation of these communities of faith to the social communities within which people live and work, and to the political systems which give structure to society? In the traditions of Western theology, philosophy and politics, this question has most influentially been framed in terms of the 'Church and State' issue. In the Muslim world, the debate has classically centred on the issue of how and through whom an Islamic society should in fact receive the guidance of Islam. Both forms of the question have been typically asked, and answers have been seminally formulated, in contexts where either Christianity or Islam elicited the allegiance of the great majority of members of society. But many societies in history, and virtually all societies today, also throw up a second, still more complex, aspect of the question – namely: How can a community of faith, in its social embodiment and attitudes, take account of a minority community that does not share the same faith?

In very different contexts, it is this second question, about community toleration of the other, which the papers in this section address. The approaches they adopt are certainly very different, but their divergence can be traced back to the very different answers each would also give to the first question, about the relation between religious communities and social structures. From his background in the Pakistani legal profession, **Dr Justice Nasim Hasan Shah** presents a robust argument for the identification of law with religion in Islamic society; on this basis, he goes on to discuss both the freedoms guaranteed to minorities in the Pakistani situation, and also the problems which they encounter. The detailed note by **Dr Mohamed El-Awa** further delineates carefully the space assigned to non-Muslims by the Qur'an and Islamic tradition. On the other hand, **Professor Michael Banner** develops a distinctively Christian case for toleration of the other on the basis of Augustine's theology, with its critique of political power built on a distinction of the 'two cities' of earth and heaven. Discussion of these complex issues shows that both Christians

48

and Muslims advocate a wide range of answers to both the questions identified above, raising issues not only about what it means to belong to human communities but also, more fundamentally, about what it means to be human beings.

Community and law: a Pakistani perspective

Nasim Hasan Shah

Pakistan: an Islamic republic

Pakistan is an Islamic state, its ideology firmly rooted in the Objectives Resolution adopted by the Constituent Assembly in March 1949. Therein it was resolved to establish such an order in Pakistan wherein the principles of democracy, freedom, equality, tolerance, and social justice as enunciated by Islam should be fully observed. For us, therefore, any mundane legal theory which is divorced from the principles of morality is not acceptable. The real aim of Islam is to obtain the sovereignty of the good, and it is our belief that this ideal can be realized through the enforcement of Islamic laws and an emphasis on the concept of morality. Religious tolerance, furthermore, is an article of our faith as it is ordained in the Holy Qur'an:

> Let there be no compulsion in religion; truth stands out clear from error. Whoever rejects evil, and believes in God, has grasped the most trustworthy handhold that never breaks. And God knoweth and heareth all things.[1]

This command for religious tolerance is fully reflected in the provisions of the Pakistani constitution, under which all people are equal before law, and are entitled to equal protection before law.[2]

However, fully to safeguard the legitimate rights of minorities further specific provisions have been made. Thus, no person attending an educational institution shall be required to receive religious instruction or take part in any religious ceremony or attend religious worship if such instruction, ceremony or worship relates to a religion other than their own. No religious community or denomination shall be prevented from providing religious instructions for pupils of that community or denomination in any educational institution maintained wholly by that community or denomination. There is to be no discrimination against any community in the grant of concession or exemption in relation to taxation in respect of any religious institution. Any religion can arrange any religious festival at any place, and anyone can participate in it even if it is of a religion other than his or her own. No citizen furthermore can be denied admission to any educational institution receiving aid from public revenues on the ground of only race, religion, caste, or place of birth, and due representation must be given to minorities in federal and provincial services.[3]

Freedom of religion in the Qur'an

These provisions are directly traceable to the verses of the Holy Qur'an guaranteeing freedom of religion – for example:

> There is no compulsion in the matter of religion.[4]

> And if thy Lord had pleased, all those who are in the earth would have believed, all of them. Wilt thou then force men till they are believers?[5]

> Had God willed, idolaters had not been idolatrous. We have not set thee as a keeper over them, nor art thou responsible for them.[6]

> If God had not raised a group (Muslims) to ward off the others from aggression, churches, synagogues, oratories and mosques, where God is worshipped most, would have been destroyed.[7]

We also find special reference being made to Christians in the Holy Qur'an:

> Nearest to you in love wilt thou find those who say 'We are Christians', because amongst these are men devoted to learning and they are not arrogant.[8]

Directing cordial social relations with other religious communities, Muslims are enjoined to deal 'kindly and justly with them for God loveth those who are just'.[9] Again, the Holy Qur'an asks Muslims to seek cooperation with the 'people of the book', i.e. Christians and Jews:

> Say, O people of the book come to common terms as between us and you. We worship none but God.[10]

Islam is the only religion which promises salvation to the followers of other religions, singling out in this regard Jews, Christians and Sabians. The Qur'an says that those who believe in God and the Day of Reckoning and do good deeds will have their reward with their Sustainer and need have no fear or grief.[11]

Again, Islam is a religion which accords the highest honour to a personage of another creed. The Qur'an devotes the highest station amongst the women of the universe to Mary (peace be upon her).[12] The Qur'an tells us that the only religion in the sight of God is Islam, that is self surrender to the will of Allah.[13] Anyone who desires something other than Islam as a religion will never have it accepted, while in the hereafter such a person will be among the losers.[14]

There should be dialogue between different faith communities, bonds of affection and friendship so that people of different faiths actually meet each other, a common effort for human well-being, as there are many issues, from matters of drug trafficking to questions of the global environment on which we can work together. It will not be easy to solve philosophical differences, but it is possible to hold to convictions with integrity while seriously engaging in dialogue. In the words of the Qur'an:

> Do not argue with followers of earlier revelation otherwise than in a most kindly manner unless it be such of them as are bent on evil doing and say 'We believe in that which has been bestowed from on high upon us, and that which has been bestowed from our God and your God is one and the same, and it is unto Him that we (all) surrender'.[15]

True religion is not a spur to confrontation or competition with other faiths. It holds out a vision that, while differences will exist in rituals and doctrines, unity is possible through dialogue in personal friendships and in work for the well-being of society.

Religion and politics in Islam

The identification of laws with religion in Muslim societies is total. Indeed, in Islam, Law is Religion and Religion is Law, because both emanate from the same source and are of equal authority, coming from the same divine revelation. The Qur'an contains for Muslims revelations which are both temporal and spiritual. These revelations cover the whole sphere of human thought and action. Being divine, they are unerring and unchangeable. Obedience to the law is thus for Muslims not a matter of ethical duty or of social expediency, but an obligation of religion itself. Life is a unity and cannot be divided into watertight compartments. Accordingly, Islam embraces within its legitimate sphere not only those acts and performances which the followers of many other religions regard as included in worship, but also aspects of individual, communal, national and international activity. The regulation of all aspects of one's life in accordance with the values of Islam constitutes a continuous worship of God. To us religion is not like a Sunday suit which can be put on when we enter a place of worship and put off when we are dealing with day-to-day life.

It is against this background that the Islamic concept of religion and the Muslim outlook on politics should be understood. Islam wants to fashion the entirety of life according to the principles of individual and social behaviour revealed by God and does not confine itself to the precincts of the private life of the individual alone. Politics, on the other hand, studies the relationship of humans with the state and with one another. In Islam this too is the domain of religion, which comprehends all aspects of life. Admitting no separation between religion and politics, Islam wants to conduct politics also in accordance with the guidance provided by religion and to effect the reformation of society. The reforms which Islam wants to bring about cannot be carried out by sermons alone; political power is necessary to achieve them. This is the basis of the Islamic approach to politics and the state.

Christians in Pakistan

The Christian and Muslim communities have been living side by side in Pakistan for centuries. Christians have been remarkable for their contributions in the area of social welfare in particular, and the services which they have offered have been widely appreciated by Muslims also.

True to the declarations of the founding father of Pakistan, Qaid-e-Azam Muhammad Ali Jinnah, the religious and human rights of the Christian community are constitutionally guaranteed. Despite the constitutional provisions, however, Christians in practice face many difficulties in Pakistan.

High posts are seldom given to Christians,[16] and no member of a minority community can become either President or Prime Minister of Pakistan. Christians and other minorities have been outside the mainstream of political life on account of the operation of the system of separate electorates. This provides for the whole of Pakistan to be counted as one constituency, with 33,000 polling booths to cover voting by Christians across the country. In practice, it is of course impossible for a Christian candidate, while contesting election to the Assembly, to make arrangements to be present or to be represented at

33,000 booths. Accordingly, the member declared as elected does not really have access to or represent the majority of his co-religionists.[17]

The sanctity of Christian marriage is also frequently violated in Pakistan. Married Christian women are either kidnapped by, or elope with, Muslim young men, who then marry them. On marriage with a Muslim man, after conversion of the woman to Islam, her previous marriage is automatically dissolved. Neither the need to seek divorce, nor the importance of fulfilling the requirement of 'idda,[18] is respected in such cases. This causes considerable anguish amongst Christians.

Pakistan's laws against blasphemy (Gustakh-e-rasūl)[19] also cause great bitterness within the Christian community. Anybody accused of defaming the Prophet can be tried for blasphemy. In most cases, claims that non-Muslims have uttered defamatory words against the Prophet, leading to their arrest and trial, are in fact false allegations, trumped up for ulterior or personal motives. The results, however, are very serious, as the alleged blasphemous words can lead to the drastic consequence of a death sentence.[20]

The difficulties faced by the Christian community are real, yet relations between the communities are generally friendly. Members of either faith participate in functions of the other – Christians celebrate 'Īd al-fitr and 'Īd al-adhā with enthusiasm alongside Muslims, while Muslims participate in Christian festivals like Christmas and Easter with equal enthusiasm. Middle-class Muslim children study together with Christian boys and girls in the numerous Christian schools throughout the country. Having been taught together by Christian teachers, they develop close ties and an understanding of each other's faiths and susceptibilities, which leads to a sense of amity and togetherness. The challenge is to make such relationships more firm, more secure, and more solid.

Response

Henri Teissier

Archbishop Teissier, speaking from his experience of living within the Christian minority in Algeria, proposed a number of questions to Muslims regarding their attitudes to people and communities of other faiths. Is there clarity in the Qur'anic position on the ahl al-kitāb, 'people of the book'? The question arises because some Muslims would apparently claim that the positive early verses were later abrogated by more negative verses.[21] Is it possible to recognize a range of Islamic opinion about the relation of religion to the state? Some today would want to see a distinction, or even a separation, between the spiritual and the temporal domains.

Should not people of faith recognize that religion is not the only factor leading to moral improvement in humanity? Much of the progress achieved in respect for human rights has been influenced by humanist thinking rather than by religious currents. Can our religious certitudes move towards greater openness towards the other? For example, many Christians now are revisiting with a more generous spirit the question of salvation for non-Christians. In fact, authentic faith itself must lead us to value and respect the other – as is evident in a letter written over a hundred years ago by Emir Abdelkader to the Bishop of Algiers:

> Whatever good we have been able to do for the Christians, we were obliged to do out of fidelity to the Muslim faith and out of respect for the rights of humanity, because all creatures are the family of God, and those most loved by God are those who are most useful to his family.[22]

Christianity, the good society, toleration and the other

Michael Banner

Toleration and Western Christians

I wish to offer some reflections concerning Christian conceptions of society, the good society, toleration and the other. I start from the thought that the question of tolerance of the other is, for Christianity in the modern West, something of an academic question. That is to say, existing under the conditions which obtain in the liberal democracies, Christianity is not called upon to make an active choice for or against toleration of other faiths (at the level of high politics, that is, however much those questions may emerge on the ground), since that toleration is required under the settlement of religious questions which emerged from the debates, disputes and wars which followed the Reformation and led up to and beyond the Enlightenment. I make the following points, however:

1. The tradition of toleration which emerged at this time and in which Western Christians operate, whatever its earlier origins, had its particular shaping and development in the seventeenth century and beyond from traditions of philosophical scepticism and radical individualism.

2. This fact creates something of an embarrassment or awkwardness for Christianity (and perhaps for Islam) in inhabiting these particular and dominant traditions.

3. Toleration in the West, which stems from this tradition, is unstable, just because its justification within this tradition is problematic.

4. Points (2) and (3) together provide Christians with reason for seeking a better basis for an understanding and account of the virtue of tolerance. This can be found, I suggest, in the Augustinian tradition, with its critique of political power as such.

5. The valuation of individual liberty which is implicit in the Augustinian tradition is compatible, however, with strong conceptions of the good and does not depend on a radical individualism; indeed it is perfectly compatible with asking questions which are often thought redundant, about, say, the character and limits of a Christian or Islamic state. Thus this way of beginning to think about the question of toleration and the other seems an appropriate place for discussions to begin between these two, or indeed other, traditions.

Toleration: the liberal tradition

1. The tradition of toleration which emerged in the West had its particular shaping from traditions of philosophical scepticism and the radical individualism which that scepticism often inspired. A line from Locke can be traced back through Hobbes and Grotius to Montaigne, and to the recovery in Montaigne of lines of thought familiar in Greek scepticism, in which all but the most minimal of moral truths were held contestable. As a result of this starting point, the project of liberal political theory in general, and of social contract theory in particular, has had a particular character: how to conceive and justify the more or less minimal state, which is the only sort of state this scepticism is generally deemed to justify. Toleration is, so to speak, an offshoot of this scepticism – since uncertainty about the good prohibited its imposition. And those who, from within this tradition, struggle for a slightly more active conception of the state (such as John Rawls) do so with their hands tied behind their backs, preventing them reaching for any richer conceptions of the good.

2. The origins of this development of toleration creates something of an embarrassment or awkwardness for Christianity (and perhaps for Islam) in inhabiting these particular and dominant traditions. First of all, Christianity may not necessarily feel at ease with at least the handling of certain forms of moral scepticism, since (except in those versions of neo-Protestantism which have become simply exhortatory rather than dogmatic) scepticism is not simply embraced. Second – and this is a related point, as we shall see – the individualism which has been so often associated with the liberal tradition sits uncomfortably with Christianity's valuation of society and solidarity (seen, for example, in the traditional critique of capitalism in Roman Catholic moral theology). Third and most important, however, whatever should be said in favour of toleration, it has, as is often noted, something of a grudging air about it. Conceptually it is generally understood as 'putting up with that which one would rather did not exist'. At the very least, Christianity will pause before adopting such a framework within which to understand other faiths.

3. To add to the hesitations provided by the last point, we should note that the practice of toleration in the West which stems from this tradition might be considered unstable, just because its justification within this tradition is problematic. As John Paul II has had cause to point out on a number of occasions, the notion that relativism favours tolerance is far from evident; the inference from 'no one can prove any moral point' to 'all moral viewpoints should be tolerated' is a faulty one. The inference is just as good (or more properly, just as bad) if the conclusion is 'therefore I may impose my values on you'. The vindication of tolerance from scepticism is, at the least, problematic.[23]

4. A better basis for an understanding and account of the virtue of tolerance, I suggest, can be found in the Augustinian tradition, with its critique of political power as such. In the next section I go on to outline this tradition and some of the developments of and reactions to it. In a short concluding section I relate this brief outline more directly to the concerns from which I began.

Toleration: the Augustinian alternative

If modern toleration is potentially unstable, Christianity may yet find itself called upon to face up to the question of toleration for itself, and specifically may have to choose for or against toleration of the religious other. Although there is a wide, varied and complex tradition of reflection within the Christian tradition which might be brought to bear on this problem, one particularly influential and important source of Christian thought about society, namely, that found in the writings of Augustine, may provide a vindication of toleration lacking in certain versions of political liberalism. Specifically, I shall suggest that Christianity, in this influential form, begins not by promulgating a conception of society, so much as by elaborating a suspicion of political power and its exercise, offering thereby a critique of political society as such. Further, though this critique may (as O'Donovan has persuasively argued) lay the foundations of modern liberalism in one sense, it differs from modern liberalism in securing the freedom of the individual not negatively, by reference to sceptical or relativistic attitudes to the good, but positively, by reference to the proper freedom of the human individual before all earthly authorities.

To the question 'where and in what form is society truly instantiated?', the Christian tradition has given a number of answers. But perhaps the most influential answer from within the Christian tradition to that question is, in brief, 'the Church', since, according to the Augustinian tradition from which this answer stems, outside that community social relations, public or private in modern terms, lack characteristics or qualities essential to them.

A dominant strand in the Christian tradition has thought about society by means of a contrast between two kingdoms, two realms or – as in the *locus classicus* of Christian social thought, Augustine's *City of God* – two cities. According to Augustine,

> Although there are many great peoples throughout the world, living under different customs in religion and morality and distinguished by a complex variety of languages, arms and dress, it is still true that there have come into being only two main divisions, as we may call them, in human society: and we are justified in following the lead of our Scriptures and calling them two cities.[24]

The two cities – the city of God (sometimes the heavenly city) and the earthly city – are to be understood as two polities, 'two political entities coexistent in one space and time', 'distinct social entities, each with its principle . . . and each with its political expression, Roman Empire and Church'.[25] But these distinct 'social entities', in virtue of their different origins, histories, and ends, are to be contrasted more starkly still; for if we must quibble with the notion that the division between the two cities is one *within society*, and note that it is actually a division *between societies*, we must also reckon with the fact that one of these is for Augustine the form, here on earth, of the one true society, whereas the other is a society only in a superficial sense. How is this so?

'The two cities', says Augustine, 'were created by two kinds of love: the earthly city was created by self-love reaching the point of contempt for God, the Heavenly City by the love of God carried as far as contempt of self.'[26] The difference in ends or objects of love creates two quite different cities: 'the citizens of each of these [two cities] desire their own kind of peace, and when they achieve their aim, this is the peace in which they live.'[27] The heavenly city, united in love of God, enjoys a peace which 'is a perfectly ordered and perfectly harmonious fellowship in the enjoyment of God and mutual fellowship in God'.[28] The earthly city also desires peace, but its peace is of a different kind. The citizens of the earthly city, in a prideful love of self over love of God, have each rejected the rule of God and chosen in preference a self-rule as intolerant of any other rule as it is of God's. For 'pride is a perverted imitation of God . . . [which] hates a fellowship of equality under God, and seeks to impose its own dominion on fellow men, in place of God's rule. This means that it hates the just peace of God, and loves its own peace of injustice.'[29] The love of self becomes, then, that *libido dominandi*, or lust for domination, which has driven the Roman Empire. Peace is achieved through the imposition of one's own will by the exercise of force, and is at once costly in its creation,[30] unjust in its character,[31] and unstable in its existence.[32]

According to Augustine, the good or value of a community lies precisely in its sociality, since it is in sociality that the human good is realized. Augustine had been tempted to represent the good life as a neo-Platonic quest with contemplation at its core. As he distanced himself from these philosophic roots, however, he came to stress the thoroughly social character of human life. Thus, though the earthly city is contrasted with the city of God, the contrast is not between the sociality of one and the asociality of the other, but rather between the doubtful sociality of one, and the true sociality of the other, a sociality with a horizontal as well as a vertical dimension. The heavenly city, united in love of God, enjoys a peace which 'is a perfectly ordered and perfectly harmonious fellowship in the enjoyment of God and *mutual fellowship in God*'.

According to Leo XIII in *Rerum Novarum*, it is the fact that sociality is a good which explains the existence of civil society in the modern sense, as well as in its older sense:

> Just as man is led by [a] natural propensity to associate with others in a political society, so also he finds it advantageous to join with his fellows in other kinds of societies, which though small and not independent are nonetheless true societies.[33]

Thus 'the natural sociability of men' is held to be the principle from which both the state and private associations are born and the good which they serve, and this prior grounding of both determines the relationship between them:

> It is by virtue of the law of nature that men may enter into private societies and it is for the defence of that law, not its destruction, that the state comes into being.[34]

In the Thomist tradition, however, this 'natural propensity' to association in society and societies has been understood as more than a tendency to mere association. Rather, it is a tendency to association in societies which presuppose and foster that community of purpose, interest, and sympathy which is expressed by the notion of solidarity. It is on the basis of such anthropological presuppositions that modern Roman Catholic social thought – from *Rerum Novarum* on through, for example, Pius XI's *Quadragesimo Anno*, and down to John Paul II's *Laborem Exercens* – has offered a critique of liberalism and socialism, which both, though in different ways, deny the naturalness of human solidarity. Free market liberalism is thought to conceive of humanity as made up of competitive individuals lacking a common good distinct from the aggregate of individual preferences. Socialism seems no less to doubt the naturalness of social solidarity, albeit that the conflictual character of society is a matter of class, rather than individual, interests and is, furthermore, not intrinsic, but is historically conditioned and contingent.

The recent *Catechism* of the Roman Catholic Church extends this analysis somewhat by finding what we might think of as a hierarchy of values in society, each serving the human good. In the first place the *Catechism* offers what seems like a pragmatic reason for 'socialization' (meaning here 'the creation of voluntary associations and institutions . . . "on both national and international levels, which relate to economic and social goals, to cultural and recreational activities, to sport, to various professions, and to political affairs"'[35]), namely that it 'expresses the natural tendency for human beings to associate with one another for the sake of attaining objectives that exceed individual capacities'.[36] In the second place, however, in mentioning again humankind's natural sociability, and thus enter-

59

taining the thought that human society is an end in itself, it goes on to connect 'socialization' with a further good:

> The human person needs to live in society. Society is not for him an extraneous addition but a requirement of his nature. Through the exchange with others, mutual service and dialogue with his brethren, man develops his potential; he thus responds to his vocation.[37]

Elsewhere it is said that the 'the vocation of man' is 'made up of divine charity and human solidarity',[38] just because 'the human person is . . . ordered to God' as well as to others.[39] The *Catechism* notes in addition, however, that 'all men are called to the same end: God himself' and that 'there is a certain resemblance between the union of the divine persons and the fraternity that men are to establish among themselves in truth and love'.[40]

The further good which might be found in human society in virtue of this 'resemblance' has been more central to Protestant thought which, if it affirms the 'natural sociability' of human kind, does so not on the basis of supposed knowledge of the natural law, but more definitely on the basis of a theological anthropology. For Karl Barth, for example, that 'the humanity of man consists in the determination of his being as a being with the other' is a counterpart of the prior fact of humankind's calling to be the covenant-partner of God.[41] Thus here the value which might be attributed to civil society is found not only in its satisfying human sociability or solidarity as such, but in the fact of this human sociability and solidarity being a likeness of, and a preparation for, the sociability and solidarity of the life of God, into which humans are called. The value of society and civil society is here firmly eschatological, we could say. The further point, however, is that this valuation of society is compatible with neither radical scepticism nor radical individualism. Where then might tolerance be learnt?

If society and civil society is thus valued, its valuation, and the critique to which it is related, indicate something of the dangers of society. In recent Roman Catholic teaching the risks associated with civil society are the risks associated with society itself, namely that higher levels of association will tend to deprive lower levels of association and individuals of their proper responsibilities. This wrong is to be prevented by respect for the principle of subsidiarity which functions as a balance to the emphasis on the common good which had been central to *Rerum Novarum*. The *Catechism* states that:

> A community of a higher order should not interfere in the internal life of a community of a lower order, depriving the

latter of its functions, but rather should support it in case of need and help to co-ordinate its activity with the activities of the rest of society, always with a view to the common good.[42]

The *Catechism* offers a theological rationale for this principle, which protects civil society against the state, but also individuals against civil society:

> God has not willed to reserve to himself all exercise of power. He entrusts to every creature the functions it is capable of performing, according to the capacities of its own nature. This mode of governance ought to be followed in social life. The way God acts in governing the world, which bears witness to such great regard for human freedom, should inspire the wisdom of those who govern human communities. They should behave as ministers of divine providence.[43]

Thus behaving, those with authority will acknowledge the existence of lower authorities and the rights of the individual, a theme which has been increasingly important in Roman Catholic social thought of the last fifty years, and which features prominently in the *Catechism* – even though there is some evidence (in *Evangelium Vitae*, for example) of a growing sense of the need to bring some order and discipline to a mode of discourse which has given us 'rights' to abortion, to die, and so on.

The Augustinian tradition, as we have seen, was suspicious of the exercise of power because of the fundamental corruption of the human will. Societies and associations, at whatever level, may provide occasions for domination and oppression. (Liberation theology is, in a sense, an heir to this tradition.) This tradition, however, has addressed and characterized the risks which societies pose, not by the formulation of an abstract principle, such as the principle of subsidiarity, nor necessarily by an elaboration of an account of human rights. Apart from anything else, to have taken this route might appear to treat the two brackets, so to speak, of the modern discussion of civil society (namely, the state and the individual in his or her privacy) as themselves autonomous and beyond criticism, when against the command of God they can possess no such autonomy. The command of God is in principle, in a manner of speaking, totalitarian.

If, however, there is a suspicion of the principle of subsidiarity and rights, it is plain enough that the totalitarian character of the rule of God itself provides a basis for a critique of all social institutions and associations, a point which was formulated with a certain clarity and force in the *Barmen Declaration* of 1934. This document can be seen as a protest at the tendency of Lutheranism, having converted Augustine's two cities into two spheres, to accord a certain independence to the state and civil society as concerned with the outer, and not the inner, life, which is the concern of the Church. In Luther's most important treatment of this matter, the distinction is used to 'safeguard religion against the unwelcome attentions of ungodly princes',[44] and thus (by the way, and to mention an occasion when Christian thought is found at the origins of civil society) provides arguments which would later be taken over almost *tout court* by advocates of religious toleration.[45] But the distinction of spheres seemed also to deny to the Church in principle the right to offer a critique of action in the public realm, even when that action involved, as here, the determination of the limits and character of society by myths of *Volk*, blood, and soil. Against such a distinction, the *Barmen Declaration* asserts that 'Jesus Christ is . . . God's vigorous announcement of his claim upon our whole life' and that 'through him there comes to us joyful liberation from the godless ties of this world', and it rejects 'the false doctrine that there could be areas of our life in which we would belong not to Jesus Christ but to other lords, areas in which we would not need justification and sanctification through him'.[46]

For O'Donovan, the modern liberalism with which Christianity may need to contend has its beginning in the Church's assertion of what he terms 'evangelical liberty', 'which is to say, the freedom freely to obey Christ'.[47] The assertion of this freedom could not but have consequences for society: 'the voice of a prophetic church in its midst, which speaks with divine authority, loosens the hold of existing authorities and evokes the prospect of liberty.'[48] For here the freedom of the individual against certain authorities is a presupposition of the assertion of the existence of yet higher authorities to which these others must themselves submit. Thus,

> Freedom . . . is not conceived primarily as an assertion of *individuality*, whether positively, in terms of individual creativity and impulse, or negatively, in terms of 'rights', which is to say immunities from harm. It is a social reality, a new disposition of society around its supreme Lord which sets it loose from its traditional lords. Yet individual liberty is not far away. For the implication of this new social reality is that the individual can no longer simply be carried within the social setting to which she or he was born; for that setting is under challenge from the new social centre. This requires she give herself to the service of

the Lord within the new society, in defiance, if need be, of the old lords and societies that claim her. She emerges in differentiation from her family, tribe and nation, making decisions of discipleship which were not given her from within them.[49]

In the early period it was perhaps the practice of avowed virginity which was the most marked sign of this freedom of decision and differentiation against authorities for the sake of a yet higher authority. But in relation to all earthly societies, the exercise of freedom, thus conceived, remains vital to Christian self-understanding, just because the ordered and differentiated society of the city which God intends is not to be identified with the imperfect societies of other cities which recognize other authorities or none.

A better toleration

For Christian thought, then, the freedom of the individual before God is the true basis of the freedom of the individual before political authorities and society. This freedom, demanded absolutely, provides, I suggest, a better starting point for theological reflection on tolerance and toleration of other faiths than does the moral scepticism and individualism of much liberal political thought. It promises not only a more secure defence of those goods, but also the basis of a better articulation of them as consisting in a patient attention to, rather than a grudging putting up with, the other.

Response

See also 'A note on Islam and other faiths' by Dr Mohamed El-Awa, pp. 65–8.

Heba Raouf Ezzat

Mrs Ezzat welcomed the emphasis on finding a rationale and a practice of religious toleration which are rooted in the core values of faith. It is important to reflect on whether Christians find that they can practise their faith better in an Islamic or in a secular context. Theological debates should be deferred to a later stage of the dialogue; the first imperative now must be to build up the experience of shared citizenship.

Probing the basis of citizenship leads to underlying questions about the purpose and character of human beings. In this respect, Augustine's thought – despite the potential of the 'two cities' approach so persuasively developed by Professor Banner – seems in some ways defective, since his understanding of what it means to be human lays a heavy emphasis on the inwardness of the self. This can lead to a tendency to withdraw from political life, particularly in the metro-political cities of contemporary capitalism, whose public space is generally hostile to the expression of religious faith and values.

Communities of human beings

The vocation to be human can only be lived out in communities of faith side by side, shaping and nurturing one another. In the West, the Christian experience of alienation from secular culture has felt threatening at times, but it has also helped to strengthen the faith of Christians. Similar challenges may be facing Islamic communities in the West soon. Some Muslims feel that there is a history here from which they can themselves learn. However, even though individual Muslims may find it congenial and even liberating, the attitude of organized Islam to any concept of autonomy based on scepticism may prove less receptive than that of Christianity.

Being a human is about either being a man or being a woman, yet differently organized communities handle these two modalities in very different ways. Many feel that neither Christian nor Muslim traditions have a good history in the ways that they have generally treated women. Any reassertion of the dominance of religion in the direction of public life would be resisted by those who fear that it would relegate women to the position of second-class citizens. There is much work of revision and reformulation for both faith communities to do in this area, and it may be possible to do some of it together.

The situations in which Christians and Muslims find themselves in many places today are such that coexistence is an established political reality, but there still remains the challenge of building up a shared history and memory of living together in community. This will involve discovering and acting on shared values. It will be moved forward by common ventures which build bridges across the gaps between the two faiths. A particularly important part can be played by the new and massively transformed spaces provided by universities, whose multi-religious and international communities could together engage in dialogue to form an ethic for the well-being of the next generation.

Most important of all is the recognition that texts and theories can only provide general, and in many ways limited, guidance in these areas. A principle of toleration can be justified by appeal to the traditions of either faith, but it can only be validated through the experience of Christians and Muslims living together in shared communities. There is a growing history of common citizenship which is being added to day by day, on which Christians, Muslims and all people need to reflect in dialogue with one another.

A note on Islam and other faiths

Mohamed El-Awa

The question of tolerance of other faiths is an essential one for Islam and for Muslim societies. Islam, being the last divine religion, had before it Judaism and Christianity as the two major divinely revealed religions. Both were practised in Arabia before Islam. Meanwhile, paganism and idolatry represented majority religious practice at Mecca, Ta'if, Medina and other famous Arab centres. Hence, the Qur'an and the practice of the Prophet Muhammad had to deal with the issue of the relationship between Islam and other faiths.

The Qur'an

While paganism was absolutely condemned – 'So avoid the filth of idols and avoid lying and false witness; turn to God, ascribe not partners unto Him'[50] – the Prophet and his followers were described in the Qur'an as believers in the revelation to Muhammad and to all previous Prophets, as well as believing in the angels and the scriptures. This faith included equality between these Prophets as Messengers of God.[51] About one third of the Qur'an is devoted to the history of the Prophet Moses and the Jewish people. Christianity as a religion, Christ as a Prophet, and the Virgin Mary are mentioned with the utmost respect whenever reference is made to them in the Qur'an.

People of all kinds and origins are called upon to 'know each other, being created from one man and one woman and made into peoples and tribes'.[52] The verb used for 'knowing' in Arabic is broad enough to include sharing life in one homeland and sharing life on earth, regardless of differences in origin and religion.

The Qur'an states[53] that Muslims, Jews, Sabians, Christians, Magians and polytheists will be subject to God's judgement in the hereafter. Another relevant verse stresses that believers who do good in this

65

world will be given their reward in the hereafter by God himself.[54] These two rulings show that the question of belief in one religion or another is not a worldly matter; it has nothing to do with people's dealings in their daily life. Rather, it is reserved to God to deal with on the Day of Judgement. The Qur'an is very clear that those who refuse to adhere to God and to accept his last revealed word will be losers in the hereafter. This must be remembered in talking about different religions and their followers: the time for solving religious differences is the Day of Judgement, when the final word will not be with any human but with the Creator of all.

Living in this world, people cannot be isolated from one another, nor can countries be reserved for one religion, with doors closed against the followers of any other. Thus, it was necessary for the Qur'an to address two kinds of human interaction. The first relates to preaching and representation of one's religion, the second to dealings between believers of different religions. For the former, the Qur'an states that calling to the way of God must be on the basis of wisdom; exhortation and exchange of views must be done in the kindest way.[55] With regard to the latter, according to the Qur'an, God does not forbid Muslims from establishing normal relationships with those followers of other religions who do not fight Muslims because of their religion, and who do not force them out of their homeland. Such normal relationships include reverence and justice, for God loves those who do justice.[56] 'Reverence' is doing good, and 'justice' is broad enough to allow every member of society, regardless of religion, to obtain rights equally with every other member. Muslims are not only allowed, but are actually ordered, to maintain reverence and justice.

Muslims are forbidden from making alliances with enemies involved in fighting other Muslims because of their religion, or supporting such fighters in forcing Muslims out of their homeland. This, though, is not from a difference in religion, but rather because those fighters and their supporters are in fact enemies of Muslim society, gathering forces under a flag of religion to fight against Muslims.[57]

On the other hand, living together in one country necessitates social mixing between Muslims and non-Muslims, and this is allowed, even encouraged, by the Qur'an itself. Sharing of food with followers of other religions – a natural result of friendly relations – and marriages of Muslim men to Jewish and Christian women are lawful.[58]

Financial dealings and trade are also allowed with the people of the book. Among those, the Qur'an differentiates between honest and dishonest people, and praises those who keep their promises and practise piety; for God loves those who are pious. Those who observe their religion are praised as believers in God and the Day of Judgement, enjoining right conduct, forbidding indecency and never delaying in good works.[59]

From this study of Qur'anic legislation related to non-Muslims, one can conclude that day-to-day living is not dependent on the religious choice of the individual, but rather on human brotherly values. This is why the Qur'an allows the establishment of all kinds of connections with non-Muslims, except for alliances with them when they fight Muslims on the basis of religion. Had it been otherwise, the Qur'an would not have ordered followers of Islam to observe reverence and justice, or allowed them to mix with non-Muslims to the extent of marrying non-Muslim women.

The practice of the Prophet

Islamic practice confirms this positive attitude to relations between Muslims and non-Muslims. Thus, the Prophet Muhammad maintained peaceful and friendly relations with the Jews of Medina until they allied against the Muslims with the pagans of Mecca, starting a war between the two parties.

Christians in particular have always enjoyed a special status, based on the Qur'anic description of them as nearest to the Muslims in affection or love.[60] This special status is well established in the *Sunna* of the Prophet. When the Christians of Najran visited Medina, he allowed them to say their prayers in his own mosque and sustained no objection to this. When a companion of his wondered why they were offering prayer with an orientation different to that of the Muslims, the Prophet ordered him to leave them to take their own direction.

One of the authentically accepted sayings of the Prophet is a *hadīth* in which he warns Muslims of causing harm to any of the people of the book, as this would be causing personal harm to the Prophet himself. When he established the first Islamic state in Medina, he dictated a constitution under which the authority of the state and inter faith relations were to be practised. Here it is clearly stated that Muslims have their own religion and Jews have theirs – a direct application of the Qur'anic rule which addressed the unbelievers by saying: 'You have your own religion and I have mine.'[61]

Dhimma

Students of Islamic jurisprudence are familiar with the concept of *dhimma* as a contract binding non-Muslims to the Islamic state in which they live. Years ago I came to the conclusion that *dhimma*, being a contract, is subject to all circumstances that may affect any contract. Some of these circumstances may bring the contract to an end, just as it was entered into in order to meet certain needs.

Dhimma as a contract came to an end at the eve of the colonial period, when foreign powers took over most Muslim lands, ending Islamic rule in these countries. The peoples of these lands, both Muslims and non-Muslims, joined in fighting the colonial presence, finally establishing modern states in various Muslim lands. In these states, citizenship in the contemporary sense has replaced the concept of *dhimma*. Since Muslims and non-Muslims have become equal citizens regardless of religion, there is no longer need to reconstitute the concept of *dhimma*. All jurisprudential references to this concept must thus be understood within their historical environment, not as a binding or eternal rule of Islamic law.[62]

In conclusion, it could be said that tolerance constitutes a pillar of Islamic faith, legislation and wisdom. For this reason, the civilization of Islam was made not by Muslims only but also by fellow believers of other faiths, in particular Christians and Jews. Followers of these religions in the Muslim world did not find any difficulty in identifying themselves with the culture of Islam, while remaining dissociated from its faith and law.

Chapter 4
Faith and change

'Change' is a profoundly paradoxical phenomenon for people of faith. On one hand, religions intend and propose radical transformations in the lives of individuals and of the world. On the other hand, religions themselves generally also find responding to change difficult at every level. As a theological challenge, this paradox is focused on the question of how to hold to faith in God as changeless in the midst of a world marked by rapid and unceasing change. Both Christians and Muslims believe that this God has revealed himself in ways accessible through space and time; how then are we to integrate revelation and response, ultimacy and immediacy, text and context? The answers we find to these theological questions will in turn inform the approaches we take to urgent practical problems of spirituality, ethics and politics in contemporary society.

The papers in this section share a concern to take seriously both the challenges posed to faith by change and the irreducible persistence of the religious witness in today's world. Using different language, they both speak of the equal need to avoid, on the one hand, an unrealistic denial of, or withdrawal from, the ever-changing reality of the world and, on the other hand, a shallow acquiescence in transience with no transcendental reference. **Professor David Ford**, reflecting in Christian terms on the experience of Europe since the Wars of Religion of the sixteenth and seventeenth centuries, concludes that the stark alternatives of 'religious' or 'secular' are both inadequate; the dynamic of faith-and-change requires us to speak rather of 'religious and secular'. **Dr Seyed Amir Akrami** gives a Muslim perspective on significant changes as they relate to religion and so to the religious guidance of society. Writing from the background of the Islamic Republic of Iran, he shows the futility of stances of either simple isolation or simple assimilation; the harmonization of faith and change requires the development of a rational and flexible jurisprudence. In a careful discussion of the philosophical and theological implications of change, the note by **Dr Christian Troll** asks specifically about the question of 'truth' and its grounding in both divine faithfulness and human freedom. Discussions of the questions of faith in the context of change, or of change in relation to faith, show Muslims and

Christians facing not dissimilar issues, albeit from different backgrounds. The three categories of 'affirmation', 'judgement' and 'transformation' might have potential as general concepts for both communities to use in responding to a changing world. At the level of methodology, there is need to develop structures of collegiality to enable Muslims and Christians to share with one another in facing parallel challenges.

Faith and change: a Christian understanding

David Ford

In a BBC broadcast last year, the Chief Rabbi Dr Jonathan Sacks said that the events of September 11 were the greatest challenge to the religions of the world since the Wars of Religion in Europe during the sixteenth and seventeenth centuries. In this paper I will start from there in order to draw from history some positive lessons about civil society and about the possibility of peace with integrity between religious traditions that have been in deadly conflict, as well as some negative lessons about secularism and about religious responses to modernity. I will suggest that there is a need to do better justice to the character of our society as 'religious-and-secular' and to the nature of healthy religious responses to modernity. Next, I will propose ten theses about Christian faith and change. I will conclude with six items for a future agenda between Christians and Muslims that might enable them to work out together better ways of drawing on the resources in their traditions for peacemaking amidst current changes.

Learning from history: a key to the relationship of faith to change

The period of the sixteenth and seventeenth centuries is a good place for a Christian and a European to start in considering 'Faith and Change'. Its religious wars played a crucial part in a transformation of Europe that involved changes which still shape our world: the development of nation states; secularization (with separation of religious from political and other institutions, and religion having less identifiable cultural influence); colonizing and imperialisms that affected most of the rest of the world; the global spread of Christianity; political, scientific, technological and industrial revolutions; constitutional democracy; and mass education. None of the world faiths has been insulated from these developments, and all have in fact changed as a result of them; but Christianity has had a uniquely direct involvement with them.

A key question in the aftermath of September 11 is therefore: what lessons can be learnt from that history? *The imperative of learning from history* is deeply embedded in Christian Scriptures. It is indeed a vital key to the relationship between faith and change. A great deal of the Old Testament is historical narrative from which lessons are continually being drawn; the prophets are concerned with discerning the meaning of the events of their time in relation to God's purposes; the wisdom literature is distilled from centuries of trying to understand personal, social and economic life with a view to human flourishing (and what prevents it); and the praising and lamenting of the Psalms are often closely related to the ups and downs of Israel's history. The New Testament pivots around the historical events of Jesus Christ's life, death and resurrection, in the light of which past, present and future are understood. Life now is lived oriented towards the kingdom of God, as portrayed in the parables of Jesus, and faithful anticipation of that requires alert responsiveness to new events, tasks, possibilities and people.

Each period of Christian history has provoked attempts to understand its meaning in the purposes of God. Perhaps the most influential in the West has been Augustine's *City of God*, written during the collapse of the Roman Empire. The greatest trauma after that was the rise of Islam, and a good deal in Medieval European and Byzantine Christianity can be understood as responding to Islam – militarily, intellectually, religiously.

Then in the fifteenth century came the Reformation and the split in Western Christianity. This was a time of vibrant Christian renewal, as well as devastating warfare which discredited Christianity in the eyes of many. The danger to which the Chief Rabbi points is that a similar discrediting, this time applying to all the conflicting religions, may be happening on a global scale now – already religion is a leading factor in many major conflicts.

But what if September 11 were to act as a shock sufficient to mobilize Muslims, Christians and others to try to avoid loss of life on the scale of the seventeenth century's Thirty Years War, and instead to find a wisdom that could contribute to a more peaceful and flourishing world in which the resources of the religions for peace are drawn upon more fully than ever before?

This Seminar could be a sign that it is possible. From both Christian and Muslim standpoints, it is better to trust that this rather than religious war is in accord with the will of a God of peace, and that the seeking of the required wisdom will be blessed by God.

But what might be the lessons of the European wars of religion?

Two positive lessons from the European wars of religion

There are two major positive lessons.

The need for civil society

One constructive and partly successful response to deadly religious conflict was to develop the institutions, laws and customs of civil society. This was in many countries as much the project of Christians who were appalled at the bloodshed in the name of their faith as it was of those who were disillusioned with Christianity as well as with war. There was collaboration among those who wanted peace through constitutional settlements, civil institutions, and distributions of power and privilege that limited the possibility of religious differences leading to international or civil war.[1] There was also resistance, refusal to cooperate, and even violence from those who wanted the settlement to be on their terms alone. But overall the advocates of civil society succeeded, and for all the debates about the quality of its civility there is a broad consensus that civil society itself has been a major contributor to the common good.

It is no accident that one of the most insistent demands since September 11 has been for what one might call a more civil global society.[2] The Chief Rabbi's challenge might be developed as follows: Can Christianity, Islam, and the often non-religious or anti-religious protagonists of contemporary capitalism[3] find the resources to weave a fabric of meaning that might shape the values, principles, agreements, laws, institutions and exchanges needed for global civil society?

The need for ecumenism

Another lesson is that it is possible for religious traditions which have engaged in deadly conflict to change with integrity and, without resolving all their differences, to live in peace with their main emphasis on conversation and cooperation. That is in fact the story of the European Churches. Its climax came in the twentieth century Ecumenical Movement.[4]

Much of the inspiration for this came from beyond Europe, but within Europe a crucial factor was the experience of total war and mass killings justified by ideologies. There are many interpretations of that movement's significance, and there have been many other factors in the transformation of Europe's religious situation.

Yet it is likely that any efforts to increase understanding and make peace between religions today would have to include elements whose worth has been shown where the Ecumenical Movement has been effective: every level – local, regional, national and international – is involved; there are bilateral and multilateral dialogues and agreements; a good deal of thorough study, discussion and publication has been essential; where the process has gone well, both leadership and extensive institutional support (including financial) have been important; and there is realism about the timescale required – divisions that developed and were reinforced over centuries need time to be understood and negotiated, and attempts to take shortcuts can be more disastrous than not engaging at all.[5]

Two negative lessons

The partial successes of civil societies and of the ecumenical movement offer resources that can lead in the direction of the wisdom needed in the present situation, but the negative lessons of the European experience also need to be learnt. These are primarily two.

The failure of secularism in a religious and secular world

First, the civility of the European settlements was extremely partial and prone to violence. Religious warfare was succeeded by imperial conquest and rivalry; French, Russian and other revolutions; and a twentieth century in which secular ideologies of communism, fascism and capitalism flourished and fought, resulting in hundreds of millions of casualties. The lesson of this is that secularism has failed even more terribly than religion.

The symbolism of September 11 was profound: it focused on the global economics of the World Trade Center and the global military power of the Pentagon (and may also have been aimed at the global political power of the White House). The main response has been in terms of military muscle and an alliance based on America's political, economic and military power. The lesson of European history and its global influence is that, whatever its short-term justification, this is unlikely by itself to lead to the peace of global civil society.

Those secular forces centred on money and arms only have access to the resources of soul, wisdom, compassion, and hope when they are set in a larger, richer fabric of meaning and purpose. One modern version of such a fabric is secular humanism with a vision of a civil, humane and just world. Desirable though that might be, it is often unaware of its dependence upon older, religiously influenced institutions, understandings and patterns of life, and has hardly yet displayed the depth, resilience and life-shaping capacity needed to form communities that can heal the divisions of our world.[6]

We have to face the religious and secular reality of our world. This reality is seen in two ways.

First, the main secular ideologies have either failed or shown their serious inadequacy, and even in crude statistical terms the vast majority of the world's population are likely to identify with one or other of the world's faiths for the foreseeable future.

Second, the secular myth of a neutral framework, with rational criteria against which to measure quality, costs and benefits (over against more partial, biased, traditional frameworks and criteria associated with religions) rightly appears less plausible than previously. Nobody has a neutral overview from nowhere, and the superiority complex of modernity in relation to religion (for all its justification in the terrible record of religion, but now balanced by a comparable secular record) can be seen as one strategy of one world-view in a bid for universality and power.

The alternative is a global civil society in which participants (including those with no religious commitment) find resources for peacemaking and serving the common good within their own traditions and through conversation and deliberation with others, and learn how to understand each other and collaborate without anyone being able to assume the role of neutral referee enforcing agreed rules. For that, intensive engagement between the participants is vital, seeking a wisdom that does justice to history and to each other as well as to their own convictions. The present seminar might be a sign that this can happen.

Inadequate religious responses

The second negative European lesson is about the failure or at least serious inadequacy of many Christian responses to the massive transformations of which the religious wars were part.

The least adequate responses are at the extremes of a continuum. One extreme allows the transformations and accompanying modern understandings to *assimilate* Christianity. This is adaptation in which nothing distinctively Christian is allowed a formative role. It is clearly inadequate from a Christian standpoint, since it evacuates Christianity of any continuing relevant content. Yet even a Christianity that is in principle against such assimilation can easily slide into it. The danger is increased by the circumstance that modern Western culture has been in closer symbiosis with Christianity than with any other faith. It may be that important lessons about alertness to assimilation and wise ways of avoiding it can be learnt by Christians from Muslims living in the West.

The other extreme attempts to prevent the transformations having any effect, preserving unchanged an earlier form of Christian faith and practice, and refusing any dialogue with modern understandings.

One form of this is attempted *withdrawal* from the modern world. The Christian critique of this questions its conception of God and Jesus Christ, its failure to affirm the goodness of creation (including many aspects of modernity), its avoidance of responsibility towards society, and its despair of possibilities of transformation for the better.

Another form tries to *fight* the modern world, dominate it, and reshape it according to its own religious vision. The Christian critique of this again relates to the conception of God and Jesus Christ, the goodness of creation, and a discerning response to modernity. In addition, there are questions about what form of communicating and spreading the gospel are in harmony with the content of the gospel and the example of Jesus Christ, and about the lessons to be learnt from the bloody history of such totalitarian religious ambitions.

Faced with extremes of assimilation to modernity or radical rejection of it, is there an alternative that has Christian integrity?

I see most types of Christianity today coming somewhere between the extremes on that continuum.[7] They try to understand Christian faith in continuity with its origins and combine it with critical and constructive engagement with modern life and understanding. Faith and change are not alternatives: the key issue is to discern how they relate to each other. There is here a wisdom that needs to be worked out afresh in each period and situation.

This is especially urgent after September 11, because most discussions have lacked a crucial category for describing reality. This is the category of a religion that is neither absorbed by modernity nor simply rejects it but is engaged in simultaneously affirming it, judging it and transforming it. If the Muslims and Christians in this seminar were to agree that this embodies the best wisdom of both of our traditions, that could be a momentous step forward. It could be the basis for intensive discussion about what is to be affirmed, and why, how, where, when, and by whom it is to be affirmed; about right judgement before God of modernity, our religious traditions, and our current situation; and about desirable transformations that follow from those affirmations and judgements and that draw on the resources of our traditions.

Christian faith and change: ten theses

What is the Christian understanding of faith and change that underlies the position being advocated: to refuse both assimilation to and rejection of modern changes; and instead to attempt to find a wisdom that appropriately affirms, judges and transforms them? I will put forward briefly for discussion ten theses on Christian[8] faith and change, any one of which could do with a paper to itself.

1. Christian faith is above all in God who is intimately involved in ongoing history for the good of the whole of creation. Creation and human history are to be paid close and appreciative attention (feeding into praise and thanks to God) as being given by God and oriented to God's glory and full life with other people before God.

2. Change can be for the better, in line with the good purposes of God, or for the worse. Human participation in history requires continual discernment, learning, and taking of responsibility in the interests of change for the better. The most serious danger is idolatry, in which what is not God is absolutized, and relations with God, other people and creation are distorted. Discerning and resisting the tendencies to idolatry, and educating desire to be non-idolatrous, are basic services to our societies.[9]

3. In Jesus Christ God has come together with the world so as to affirm radically its created goodness, to judge its sin and evil, and to transform it into the kingdom of God. Jesus Christ was involved with change for the better and for the worse. The threefold realism of affirmation (seen especially in his ministry of healing, feeding, teaching, etc.), judgement (especially in his death), and transformation (especially in his resurrection) embodied in the crucified and risen Jesus Christ is at the heart of Christian involvement with change in history.[10]

4. The Holy Spirit 'poured out on all flesh' is the continuing eventfulness of God in history, opening it up to God's purposes and enabling ongoing affirmation, judgement and transformation.

5. Christians are called to be affirmed, judged and transformed by God through Jesus Christ for the sake of the affirmation, judgement and transformation of the world. This calling centres on their participation in the worshipping community of the Church.

6. With regard to the massive changes associated with modernity, there is a demanding task of wise discernment, accompanied by efforts, in collaboration with others, to heal both the religious traditions and modernity. Essential to Christian discernment is continuing conversation around Scripture, drawing on the resources of tradition, the world-wide Christian community and the world-wide academic community. The indwelling of Scripture through worship, prayer, study, the arts, academic disciplines, discussion, debate, and living in the world in faith is at the heart of lively Christian wisdom in response to change.

7. In relations with Muslims, whose own scriptures are likewise vital to discernment with regard to faith and change, any worthwhile mutual understanding will have to include sharing in the processes of scriptural interpretation (and the responses to historical developments involved in that) in both traditions. There should also be participation in this by Jews, as the eldest siblings of the Abrahamic faiths. Such intensive, long-term conversation around seminal texts while seeking wisdom for the contemporary world is a model of how to ensure that participants in a pluralist situation (including others besides Jews, Christians and Muslims) engage with each other at a level that allows for the discovery of shared wisdom.

8. Institutions, organizations and other structured focuses of life in society are vital arenas for facing the challenges of modernity (together with many serious challenges that have little to do with modernity). In line with my analysis of the importance of civil society in our religious and secular world, these must become places where religious resources for peace and flourishing are available. What is the potential for this in national and local government, the health service, business, the judicial system and prisons, education, the media, entertainment, and so on?

9. Part of the task of collaborative discernment and healing is to do with modern knowledge, its applications, and its institutions. Universities in particular are places where Christians, Muslims, those

of other faiths, and those identified with no faith come together in learning, teaching, scholarship and research with responsibilities in relation to students, knowledge, understanding and applications that are vital to the shaping of our world. At present many universities in the West (and elsewhere too) are strongholds of secularism. If they are to contribute constructively to understanding and peace in a religious and secular world they need to become religious and secular universities, where there can be sustained engagement with questions of truth and practice raised by, between and about the world's religions.[11]

10. Human history and achievements, together with society and its institutions, should not be seen as ultimates. They are penultimate; God and God's kingdom alone are ultimate, and the beginning of wisdom is to recognize this. *Realizing the right relation of the ultimate to the penultimate is at the heart of wise living.* A wrong emphasis on the penultimate can lead to compromising Christian faith, to assimilation, and to idolatry. An emphasis on the ultimate out of right relationship to the penultimate leads to fanaticism, religious warfare, and other forms of idolatry. Jesus Christ is neither compromiser nor fanatic, but lives affirming, judging and transforming the penultimate sphere while also orienting it towards ultimate transformation.[12] His followers are called to live in that dynamic, their basic act being to recognize the ultimacy of God through worship and through prayer for the kingdom of God. One important penultimate goal in the present situation is a non-idolatrous, religious and secular civil society.

Items for a future agenda between Christians and Muslims

The events of September 11 have already produced considerable changes. In the light of the above understanding, what sort of agenda between Christians and Muslims might now help to generate further changes for the better?

1. *The ultimacy of God.* In what ways can the horizon of a God of peace, wisdom and compassion be shared by Christians and Muslims? Can we identify what in the relations of Christians and Muslims, and in their relations with others, most fully glorifies God? How can we help each other to be faithful to God in the current testing of our capacity for wisdom, peacemaking and compassion? What practices of prayer for each other should each adopt? How do we handle the fact that Muslims and Christians identify God very differently?

2. *Affirmation, judgement and transformation.* Can Muslims and Christians collaborate in trying to find a wisdom of affirmation, judgement and transformation in relation both to each others' traditions and practices and to the developments of modernity? In dealing with modernity, is it right to avoid both extremes of assimilation and outright rejection? If so, how can this best be done by each community and by both in collaboration?

3. *A non-idolatrous religious and secular civil society.* Is this the right interim goal, given the lessons of history and the present world situation? If so, how can it best be developed by Christians, Muslims and others, both nationally and internationally?

4. *Forms of collegiality for seeking and sharing wisdom.* If the above items are to be taken seriously, appropriate groups, settings, structures and procedures are needed to enable Christians and Muslims to study, discuss, deliberate, and decide together. One concern which might be built into all wisdom-seeking (as it is into this Seminar) is to explore the possibility of agreeing on common and truthful descriptions of each community and its history and present situation. Christians and Muslims each have well-developed internal forms of collegiality, but almost no joint collegiality. This is the greatest single practical lack in the present situation between the two. What forms might joint collegiality take? Who might initiate them? How might they be resourced? What might Christians and Muslims need to learn from each other,[13] and what might both of them learn from other traditions?[14] What are the most stubborn issues, and how can they be faced? Is such collegiality fatally undermined by the missionary nature of each faith, or are there ways to have both collegiality and missionary integrity?

5. *Signs of Muslim–Christian service of the common good.* How might Muslims and Christians collaborate in serving the common good in every area of life? Instead of living up to the image of religion as causing division and conflict, how can they together serve peace, justice, the flourishing of civil society, and the seeking and sharing of wisdom for the common good? The aim should be to create signs of peacemaking in each sphere – politics, business, law, education, the media, and so on. What are the priorities here?

6. *Movements, networks, institutions, groups, friendships: the issue of scale.* The problems and possibilities between Christians and Muslims are so profound and extensive that it is unlikely that anything less than a movement (cf. the Ecumenical Movement discussed above), or even more than one movement,[15] would be able to have the desired impact.

It is also possible to imagine networks, institutions and groups, with the face to face level being crucial if the essential element of trust is to be built up. But it is probably wise that there should be no master-plan. Perhaps the main lesson of the Ecumenical Movement is that it began in friendships. The most challenging question is: Are Muslims and Christians open to the friendships that God is inviting them into today?

Response

Tariq Ramadan

Professor Ramadan pointed out the difficulties of living practically by faith in the European context. A Muslim's central motivation is directed towards the ultimacy of God. The aim is to please him, not other people, yet listening to and understanding others – sometimes even being in conflict with others – can assist the fulfilment of Islam. It should not be expected, though, that the Islamic experience will necessarily mirror that of Christianity, particularly in thinking about the scriptures in relation to change.

Muslim communities around the world find responding to change problematic; some of this is due to a series of prevalent confusions. For example, Islamic principles need to be distinguished from ethnic cultures, and universal principles should not be conflated with a variety of particular models through which they might be realized. It is simplistic to assert that there is 'no difference' between religion and politics, since this blurs the line between prescription and openness; similarly, the Sharī'a should not be seen just in terms of prohibition and limitation, but as a positive way to remain faithful to Islam. In the West, Muslims and Christians are both in some sense cast in minority roles, and a dialogue between them needs to begin on an equal footing. It is misleading to identify universal values solely with Western values – the Qur'an also offers universal values.

Affirmation, judgement, transformation

The categories of affirmation, judgement and transformation can be helpful in describing how faiths respond to any episode of change in their context – it does not seem that the situation of modernity is qualitatively different in this respect. For Christians and Muslims, though, affirmation, judgement and transformation need to be rooted in the priority of God, not in the human attitudes which we happen to bear towards one another.

The formula of 'affirmation-judgement-transformation', although it can be related to Christology, is also congruent with the Islamic idea of 'reform', and this opens up the possibility of Christians and Muslims working together in a number of areas to apply the witness to the divine challenge addressing a world of change. Examples would include the status of women, the development of civil societies, and justice in the relationship between North and South. Modern globalizing capitalist societies create public spaces which are inherently hostile to the development of inter faith partnerships for judgement and transformation; Christians and Muslims need to form alliances together to reaffirm God-given values in these places. In this context, it is also important to be aware of both the dangers posed and the opportunities offered to inter faith cooperation through the development of worlds of electronic virtual reality.

Islamic responses to change

Seyed Amir Akrami

In this paper, I shall first introduce the issue of 'change' in the understanding of different religions, then deal briefly with some of the major changes that have taken place in the modern world. In the third part, I will examine how Muslim, especially Iranian, religious scholars have dealt with these changes and the challenges they raise.

Change and religion

The traditions of the various theistic religions provide their adherents with a fund of teachings, doctrines, narratives, images and injunctions in terms of which they interpret the nature of God and God's relationship with the world and with themselves, and the ways in which they are to overcome meaninglessness in their lives and in the world in fellowship with God. Although all theistic believers claim that God alone is worthy of ultimate devotion, the differences between the interpretative frameworks provided by their various religious traditions can cause them to differ in their understanding of the nature of God and of the devotion which is due to God, the purposes of God which direct their actions and bestow meaning on events in the world, the ways in which they can overcome meaninglessness and become reconciled with God, the forms of spirituality in which they express their relationship with God and through which they train themselves to understand their lives and the world in theistic terms. However, these differences exist not only between religious traditions but also within the same tradition. Even within the same tradition, such as Islam or Christianity, believers may differ widely among themselves in their interpretation of these points, and may even hold widely different views on the nature of God. In fact, the differences between Muslims and Christians are in many ways less than those within either the Christian or the Muslim tradition. Religious traditions are not monolithic and immutable systems of thought; they allow for various ways of understanding the meaning and significance of life and the world.

Moreover, this plurality is found not only between believers at any given time, but also between believers through the course of history. A religious tradition is a process in which religious faith is handed down from one person to another, and from one generation to the next. In a process of socialization, believers receive from the past a heritage in the form of rites, ideas, vocabulary, stories, images and metaphors, social institutions and so on. This heritage includes the totality of forms in which their predecessors had expressed in thought and action the faith which they in turn had received from their predecessors. What past generations handed down in this way, though, is not identical with what they received. By making the faith their own and by expressing it authentically in ways which are relevant, adequate, intelligible and credible in their own circumstances, they added their own form to it. In the same way, the present generation of believers will hand down the religious heritage which they have received in a modified form to those who come after them. Thus, a religious tradition is a cumulative process of interactions between the religious heritage which is handed down and the personal faith of those who make this heritage authentically their own. The heritage which has been handed down does not include the later expressions of faith. On the contrary, these are added to it cumulatively. So the faith of later generations is conditioned by the heritage but not completely determined by it. The personal faith of every believer adds his or her own authentic expression to it. The later history of the tradition is thus the prolongation and enrichment of its earlier existence as modified by the intervention of the personal faith and activities of countless members of the community of believers.

Changes in the modern world

Let me give some instances of changes which have affected the Islamic tradition in the modern world. The rise of the natural sciences has caused many changes in understanding of the scriptures. A simple example of this is the interpretation of Qur'anic passages related to meteors. Some verses in the Qur'an teach that God sends down meteors in order to prevent Satan from entering heaven.[16] In his commentary on these verses, 'Allāmah Tabātabā'i, one of the most brilliant Shi'ite thinkers and exegetes, writes that, because of new findings in natural science which explain how these meteors are sent down, we can no longer accept the traditional interpretation of these verses which understands them in a literal way. Rather, they must be interpreted metaphorically and symbolically.[17] This is a theoretical example, but Muslim thinkers have also had to face practical problems and challenges in the modern world. Well-known examples are those relating to the consistency of democracy with Islamic teachings on governance and human rights, especially women's rights.

The 'modern world' is not only modern because of new technological devices such as aeroplanes, computers and so on. These are themselves the results of basic changes in our way of understanding the world. In the first place, unlike the thinking of pre-modern philosophers, the prevalent way of thinking in the modern world – due especially to Kant's philosophy – takes into consideration the limits of human reason in the process of knowledge, within which intentionality and action play a major part.

Another major change comes from the sociology of knowledge, which emphasizes the important role of the cultural and geographical background of our thought. Karl Mannheim, for example, laid stress on the fact that our knowledge is 'standpoint-bound'.

A third major shift is in the attention paid to the limits of language. The work of Austin and Wittgenstein revolutionized the philosophy of language, and many subsequent thinkers have come to understand that all statements about the truth of things can necessarily be at most only partial descriptions of the reality they seek to describe: although reality can be seen from many perspectives, human language can express things from only one, or a very few, perspectives at the same time.

A fourth major influence on the structure of modern thinking has come from hermeneutics, with its claim that all knowledge of a text is an interpretation of it. This basic insight, though, goes beyond textual knowledge: all knowledge is seen to be interpreted knowledge, and the knower is part of the known – especially, but not only, in the disciplines of the humanities.

A final important change in the modern mentality has been a realization of the historical context of our knowledge. In the nineteenth century, many scholars came to perceive all statements about the meaning of something as being partially products of their historical circumstances. Those concrete circumstances helped to determine the fact that the statement under study was called forth in the first place, and that it was couched in particular intellectual categories, literary forms and psychological settings.

All these important and major changes in the modern world – which I have referred to only in an incomplete and somewhat superficial way – clearly indicate that our ways of thinking and of acquiring knowledge have experienced dramatic changes. The shifts I have mentioned are of a theoretical nature, but they have great practical consequences. Besides these theoretical changes, or paradigm shifts, there have also been more practical changes such as those in the understanding of human rights, especially the rights of women and of minorities. I now wish to examine how these dramatic changes have been encountered by Muslim thinkers.

Muslims encountering change

Approaches taken by Muslim scholars and thinkers in response to these changes and challenges can be classified into three main groups.

1. There are those who deny any sort of change, or who think that a traditional understanding of religion is sufficient for tackling the problems of today's world; they insist that it is not necessary to change or to modify this understanding of religion. For such scholars, the only source of knowledge is the Qur'an and the *Hadīth*; they do not take seriously the findings of human reason in the various branches of natural sciences and the humanities. For this group, it is not religious knowledge which is problematic, but rather our world that has to change in order to be consistent with our understanding of religion. This could be described as a position of isolation.

2. Others, by contrast, think that the solution to the problem is to ignore the religious tradition or heritage, or try in some way to dispense with it. According to this group, that heritage can no longer provide us with appropriate and adequate ideas to enable us to deal with the problems of today's world. Clearly this is not a religious

approach, and so cannot be acceptable to religious people. It could be described as a position of assimilation. While the first group denies change, this second group rejects the religious tradition, and so they too cannot offer an appropriate way of harmonizing faith and change.

3. A third group – which includes within it various interpretations (as do the first two) – takes account of the changes I have described, recognizing that these are so important that our understanding of Islam cannot remain the same. It is neither possible nor desirable to maintain the same Islamic teachings that our predecessors held a millennium ago. Within this group, the question then arises of the extent to which our understanding of religion can change. In other words, how can we maintain that the various and changing conceptualizations of faith within the tradition are all forms or expressions of *the same* faith?

> The difficulty arises from the conviction of believers that the message proclaimed in their tradition is God's definitive word to mankind. Therefore, unless the word proclaimed to men [sic] of every successive age and culture is in some significant sense the same word, God's promise is not fulfilled.[18]

These words clearly show how delicate and difficult is the task of the re-interpretation of religion in order to deal with change. To this question two major responses have been given within the Islamic scholarly community.

Some Muslim scholars think that traditional methods of *ijtihād* can successfully address the challenges of the modern world. The experience of the Islamic Republic of Iran, however, clearly shows that this way of dealing with the problem is not satisfactory. Even for a high-ranking traditional jurist (faqīh) such as Imam Khomeini, 'the prevalent *ijtihād* in Islamic seminaries is not sufficient . . . and time and place must play a role in the process of *ijtihād*'. It is noteworthy that the main reason behind this shift in his thought was that, after coming to power, he realized that he was faced with many practical challenges which could not be solved by the traditional *ijtihād*. That is why in Iran's system of legislation there are three main centres: the Parliament, which tries to find solutions from a practical point of view; the Council of Guardians, which examines whether or not laws passed in the Parliament are in line with the Sharī'a and Constitution; and the Council of Expediency, whose decision is overriding when there is any disagreement between the two. It is clear that in this process the arbiter is human reason, which is the source of the Expediency Council's decisions. This mechanism can in principle bring about drastic changes in *ijtihād*, as can be seen from the following more detailed consideration.

Islamic jurisprudence is usually divided into three major parts: (1) injunctions and prohibitions related to worship, such as prayer (*salāt*), fasting, alms and pilgrimages; (2) those related to transactions; and (3) those related to governance, such as allegiance, consultation, punishment, retaliation, blood-compensation, and general guardianship. A historical study shows that all these parts have never been mysterious, and there have always been clear explanations for all of them. That is why al-Ghazali and al-Shatebi argued that all Islamic jurisprudence aims at preserving five main things ('five purposes', *al-maghased al-khamsa*): religion, reason, blood relationship, property and life. Another principle in Islamic jurisprudence states that whatever is confirmed by reason is confirmed by religion, and vice versa. On the other hand, one of the main sources of Islamic jurisprudence is reason. All these considerations, therefore, raise the question to what extent today's *ijtihād* is moving in a rational direction.

It seems that, generally speaking, no major changes are needed with respect to matters concerning (1) worship and (2) transactions. With regard to issues of (3) governance, however, the situation is different. If the basic procedure in jurisprudence is to find solutions to problems, it is necessary first to clarify what those problems really are. Current world problems do pose some questions for Islamic jurisprudence, among which I shall refer to just two – one concerns the penal law, and the other relates to the system of governance. With regard to penal law, the question is whether or not this system is able to prevent the occurrence or spread of crimes in a given society. With regard to the system of governance, the question is how to achieve a just government. Is democracy one way of reaching this goal, and is it in line with an Islamic kind of government? When we pursue questions like this, we see that the prevalent answers given by Muslim jurists do not respond appropriately to the situation. Thus a fundamental question arises as to whether those teachings in Islamic jurisprudence which are used as sources for answering these kinds of questions can in fact be used for addressing the challenges of our times.

Upon closer, and especially historical, examination, it becomes clear that the sources or texts addressed problems of the time of the Prophet, and were appropriate attempts to create a moral and just society at that time. For example, the laws relating to retaliation and punishment were aimed at controlling the dominant violent tendency of those people. If one person from a tribe was killed, many people would be killed from the other tribe in retaliation. In such circumstances, the Prophet tried to control the situation by saying that only one person could be killed in retaliation. In the Qur'anic verses dealing with this question, it can be clearly seen that retaliation is used in contrast with aggression, and that it is considered a mercy. In addition, people were asked to forgive the criminal. These points indicate that the main purpose was moral, rather than to establish a permanent legal system. From these facts, it can be inferred that what the Prophet said and did should be regarded as pointing to the direction in which to follow, rather than as the final point to which we should adhere forever. In the deeds and words of the Prophet, we find a general orientation towards justice and mercy; the laws he laid down for that time cannot be considered permanent and final.

Similar considerations apply to the system of government in Islam. The Prophet tried to establish a just government in his time, but in our time Muslim scholars should try to find the best kind of political system – one which is just in the sense that it more adequately distributes power, and prevents injustice, oppression, corruption and poverty. This system might structurally be different from the political system of the time of the Prophet, but that is not important. What is important is to see whether or not justice, as defined today, can be obtained through this system. In recent years, there has been much discussion as to whether democracy is consistent with Islam. The above analysis can tenably show that, if this system is the best way of achieving justice among current rival systems, then it is consistent with Islam. The great Muslim intellectual of Pakistan Muhammad Iqbal said: 'Islam asks us to be loyal and faithful to God, not to dictatorship.'[19] It is a duty for all Muslim intellectuals to define the meaning of justice for today, to try to find its various instances in different areas of life, and to put it at the basis of any attempt at establishing an Islamic society. Not only is this not in opposition to God's will, it is exactly what God wants us to do.

I have given a historical interpretation of Islamic jurisprudence. As Iqbal says, this type of interpretation or reconstruction is needed due to basic changes in the political, social and cultural conditions of Muslim societies in the modern world. I have tried to argue that a desirable consistency between religious teachings and the realities and challenges of today's world cannot be achieved simply through *ijtihād* in minor things. What is required is *ijtihād* in major things, or in some principles. By giving a more prominent role to human reason, which according to Islamic tradition is our internal witness to God and which constitutes a source of Islamic jurisprudence, it seems possible to find ways of reconciling Islam with the challenges of the modern world. Of course, this does not mean that Islam – or any other religious tradition – can accept all types of change. As Iqbal says: 'It is our duty cautiously to observe the progress of human thought and constantly to take an independent critical approach towards it.' The task of harmonizing religious values with the challenges of the modern world is a difficult one; I have offered just a modest attempt in this direction.

Response

Christian Troll

See further Dr Troll's 'A note on the question of truth', pp. 89–94.

Dr Troll pointed to the importance of the debate about change taking place within Islam today. Answers are being sought in a reconstruction of the Sharī'a through a revitalized *ijtihād* which goes back directly to the revealed texts. This implies looking beyond the details of a unified system of law to ask about underlying principles. In the terms of Islamic jurisprudence, this is an investigation of the *maqāsid*, 'goals and objectives', of divine directives. In the area of political matters, the *maqsad* is essentially the realization of the justice which God wills.

While the current context presents these challenges of *ijtihād* with a particular immediacy, the form of the question is not in itself new in Islam. The jurisprudential tradition has elaborated discussions about the role of reason in relation to revelation in arriving at a sense of direction, about the way in which a community consensus can be reached, about the status of such a consensus in binding believers, and so on. One pressing issue which does require more extended consideration is that of the question of revelation, truth and historical change.

Developing Muslim–Christian collegiality in the face of change

Given that Muslims and Christians are both facing significant challenges in their faiths in relating to change, in particular in accommodating the reality of pluralism, it is vital to nurture relationships which enable them to address these issues in partnership. Such structures of collegiality already exist to some extent, but they need to be multiplied and strengthened. The missionary nature of both faiths, and the fears or suspicions this can engender, can sometimes make a sense of collegiality more difficult.

Building in an appreciation of the other is particularly important in the formation of religious leaders. For example, those training as Shi'ite clerics in Iran are being encouraged to study overseas in non-Islamic contexts. In some cases, the official reason for this may be to learn to criticize errant ways of thought; yet the reality of engagement with another tradition may in fact engender a more positive attitude. Similarly, the missionary and apologetic motives in Christianity have led to a dialogical involvement issuing in a deeper appreciation of Islam. A major challenge for the future is to find ways of extending these experiences, so that, for example, it becomes normal for Christians or Muslims training as religious leaders to receive accurate and sympathetic instruction on Islam or Christianity respectively. This should aim in the first place to generate an understanding of the other in a way that matches the other's self-understanding, rather than viewing them through categories entirely bounded by one's own tradition. Beyond the formation of religious leaders, there then spreads out the still wider task of nurturing an appreciation of the other at grassroots level in both communities.

A note on the question of truth

Christian Troll

This note adverts to one question that, in the area of faith and change, is crucial with regard both to Islamic and Christian thought: that of the claim to truth which each tradition makes in face of the not yet concluded understanding of faith. In his critique of religion, Friedrich Nietzsche (1844–1900) reproaches Christianity as well as Islam for having fostered an attitude convinced that only the others can learn from my own one true and revealed religion. The other religion may well possess deep and beautiful thoughts, truths and elements of truth, but these are found in one's own religion as well. In the last analysis therefore, it is superfluous to listen to the other; one's own knowledge in faith is sufficient to itself.

Nietzsche illustrates the point with the following anecdote. After the conquest of Alexandria (642), Caliph 'Umar was asked by his general how to proceed with the powerful and famous library of that city. 'Umar is said to have given the succinct order: 'If the books agree with the Qur'an, the word of God, they are superfluous, and there is no need to preserve them; in case they do not, they are dangerous; you should order them to be burnt.' Nietzsche comments tersely: 'That was how the Catholic Church thought with regard to Greek literature.'[20]

Historically this anecdote, and Nietzsche´s comment upon it, can easily be critically challenged. Yet, however exaggerated the formulation of his criticism, it seems that Nietzsche has a point relevant to a proper self-understanding of both Christianity and Islam: neither religion has found it easy to admit the need of a continuous effort to learn from, and with, those who take another viewpoint, so as to be able to act together with them too.

The Roman Catholic Church, for example, from the Middle Ages onwards increasingly began to define itself as a *societas perfecta* – comparable to the state – 'a self-sufficient society not depending on any other authority, disposing of all legal possibilities and facilities for ordering and securing the common life of all people united in her'.[21] Obviously, such a self-understanding was not without consequences. The Church, for centuries, not only aimed at defending herself against external encroachments of state power, but also tried to preserve exclusively for her 'spiritual authority' the final competence to judge all human affairs. Only with the Second Vatican Council did the Roman Catholic Church, officially as well as comprehensively on the normative level, arrive at another attitude and mode of discourse. In doing so she reacted, however late, to a societal situation marked by ideological and religious pluralism, forcing her to rethink her own heritage of faith. Especially significant is the way in which the documents of Vatican Council II evince a fresh consciousness that, in the fulfilment of her duty, she has in a way to depend on the 'world' in its cultural and religious diversity.

The Council, taking up the call by Pope John XXIII to decipher God's will for her in the signs of the time, stated that 'in the presence of this vast enterprise [i.e. the coming into being of a single interrelated world-wide community], in which the whole human race is now involved, the Church sees herself not only as not having always a ready answer to particular questions', but furthermore foresees expressly that 'the light of revelation combines with universal experience, so that illumination can be forthcoming on the direction which humanity has recently begun to take'.[22] In this she attributed 'to earthly realities in our world an autonomy in the sense that they have their own laws and values', and was asked to acknowledge such autonomy of created realities 'as not only demanded by people today, but as in harmony with the will of the Creator'.[23] The fact that the Council did not attempt to 'define the interpenetration of the heavenly and earthly cities' but rather declared it 'the mystery of human history'[24] shows how little it intended to separate or delimit the one part from the other. The Church here was fully aware of 'how much it has received from the history and development of the human race'. And it deemed that in the future, too, 'such an exchange' would be to her own advantage.[25]

Although, with regard to the other religions, there was an avoidance of any suggestion that the Church could learn truly new things from alien cultures and religions, yet the consciousness expressed – that humanity (of which the Church forms a part) is on the way to a 'universal culture' – pointed to an openness of great possible conse-quence, far beyond that which the Fathers of the Council may have foreseen. In any case, the declarations of an ecumenical Council are in large measure programmatic and visionary in nature. They should be read as expressions of intent rather than of a given reality. Though the Church's move beyond its own frontiers in no way guarantees that a corresponding spiritual and intellectual climate has actually come about within it, yet the task has been authoritatively and irreversibly indicated and legitimized by no less authority than an ecumenical Council. Analysis of post-conciliar statements and initiatives of the Holy See and regional bishops' conferences provides rich evidence that the Church today accepts, even promotes, the living exchange of religious experience as a process of mutual cleansing and enriching.[26]

It would certainly be inappropriate to draw conclusions from the learning process of one religion (even less one church) for possible developments in other religions, for instance Islam. But in the measure that the various cultures in the process of encountering one another not only exchange single elements but rather develop shared normative standards – for instance in the field of ethics and politics through human rights, in that of the sciences through regulated procedures of the control of knowledge – a basis for understanding and action takes shape that extends beyond the more limited area of influence of one given religion. Thus they may be challenged to examine whether this area cannot be further extended and consolidated.

Let me take as an example the elaboration of Islamic human rights thinking by certain Muslim organizations during the past decades. Human rights as formulated in the United Nations Declaration of 1948 were conceptualized after manifold political and ideological disputes in a given historical situation and epoch – the European enlightenment of the eighteenth century. In the view of most Muslims, this deprives them of any truly universal validity and claim. In fact, most Muslim believers would think that someone wanting to arrive at basic rights should seek and find them, where they are already and always given: in the Qur'an and Sunna. According to such thinking, all discussions in the West concerning human rights are no more than the expression and consequence of ignorance.

The introduction to the 'Universal Islamic Declaration of Human Rights', adopted in 1981 by the International Islamic Council,[27] seems to give expression to this view: 'Islam gave to mankind an ideal code of human rights fourteen centuries ago.' Behind this statement we detect a consciousness that adherence to human rights, in so far as they take as their foundations other sources than the Qur'an, and which as to their capacity to find consensus among non-Muslims may be superior to it, could severely damage one's own foundation of faith. In that case, a legal foundation could be assumed to exist and be credited with universal validity which is in no way legitimized in the religious law, and which furthermore is not identical with it as to content. A separate Islamic Declaration of Human Rights represents, therefore, an attempt on the one hand to support the modern effort towards legal protection of human dignity by means of one's own for-mulation, but on the other hand equally an attempt to counteract from the outset any possible qualifying of the Qur'an and Sharī'a. However, one may be forgiven for estimating that the claim will not find acceptance beyond the limits of the Muslim community. If, in the 'explanation' added to the English version of the text, it is stated that throughout 'the term "Law" denotes the Sharī'a, i.e. the totality of ordinances derived from the Qur'an and the Sunna and any other laws that are deduced from these two sources by methods considered valid in Islamic jurisprudence', then this amounts to a delimiting explana-tion with far-reaching consequences. For example, Article 13 of the Universal Islamic Declaration, dealing with religious freedom, assures 'every person the right to freedom of conscience and worship in accordance with his or her religious beliefs'. What it does not state clearly is that it remains absolutely forbidden for Muslims to turn their back on their own religious community in order to join another one.

Differences between the modern understanding of fundamental rights and that which is orientated to Muslim tradition are quite obstinate. According to general Muslim understanding, on the one side stands the absolute wisdom of God, and on the other merely the insufficient and time-conditioned efforts of humans towards a political order. Is it correct to conclude that in the situation described here both religions are exposed to the pressure of the prevailing social conditions affecting them equally? Comprehensive social realities would seem to render one single religion insufficient for providing basic orientations for shared action. The partners in plural society are 'forced' to look out for foundations more likely to make possible an agreement for shared living in diversity. The predicament of modern societies, frequently designated in a summary way as 'secularization', seems to have been caused primarily not by a non-religious cultural mentality, but rather by the necessity to find a wider social basis than one particular culture and religion can offer.

It would certainly be unrealistic in the given circumstances of our world to presume that one single religion will be able in the foreseeable future to provide the basis for a free agreement of the different peoples and cultures or of the different groups in our plural global society. However, it does not seem equally unrealistic to try finding beyond all the divergences a growing consensus in more general human orientations – and there would seem to exist good reasons for arriving together at judgements with a claim to absoluteness, especially as to what should be removed from our world as evil. In this situation, the religions are challenged to elaborate together the ways in which they can and should make their specific contributions, under circumstances largely indifferent to their special claims to validity of faith.

For Islam too, this raises difficult questions. Islam's tendency to conceive of religion and society as overlapping realities stands in such a diametrically opposed relationship to a secularized world that a solution is hard to discern. However, I am not concerned here with predicting historical developments and putting forward moral duties; I merely want to point to that fact that the various religious traditions in the modern world – precisely with regard to those elements prescribed as unconditional religious obligations – will increasingly weaken in their functioning, even to the point of dysfunctionality, unless they can base certain convictions on a broader consensus than one single religious community can provide.

Christianity and Islam are both affected by this situation. Their credibility in the eyes of outsiders seems decisively to depend upon how far they manage to accept creatively their fate of being, in a sense, *de facto* qualified, without emotionally evading the realization of this fact by fostering a consciousness of being in an absolute way 'the final truth'.

Chapter 5
Setting the agenda

How can Christians and Muslims together identify and act on an agenda for the future? Given the very diverse situations around the world in which people of the two faiths are living and encountering one another, there will clearly be a number of different kinds of answer to this question. Some will focus on the dynamics of one particular national or regional context. Others will seek to identify common themes around the world. The first two papers in this chapter exemplify these two approaches. **Dr Rabiatu Ammah** writes out of her context as a West African Muslim woman, paying particular attention to issues of Islamization as they affect Christians as well as Muslims. **Professor Tarek Mitri**, from his extensive experience in the World Council of Churches, draws out recurrent problems and opportunities from across the range of Christian–Muslim dialogues today.

It is not only the interplay of local diversity and global commonality that makes the discernment of future agendas so difficult. The papers collected here have touched on a wide range of issues in a number of different spheres of exchange – the dynamics of coexistence and co-citizenship of Christians and Muslims; their historical experiences of relationship and failure of relationship; the theological and spiritual challenges raised by their mutual encounter; the opportunities encouraging them towards, and the limitations holding them back from, the creation of new worlds together. The second pair of papers try to gather together some of this sharing across so many areas. **Bishop Michael Nazir-Ali** points to some of the ways in which Christians and Muslims can look forward to working jointly on key issues. **Professor Gillian Stamp** offers a reflection on the different levels and interlocking processes of meeting and exchange which the Lambeth seminar drew into its task of 'building bridges' between the two faiths.

Whenever Christians and Muslims meet in a spirit of openness and honesty in today's world, they will necessarily be aware of how many are the issues which face them together, and how few are the areas which any discussion can realistically cover. Some of the priorities identified for further work together involve theological and philosophical dialogue; others require common action with a pressing sense of urgency. Both types of issue point to the enormous energy present in the meeting of Christians and Muslims today, and to the need to extend opportunities for meeting to wider circles of people in both faiths.

Building God's peace and justice together

Rabiatu Ammah

This paper will focus on a critical assessment of the position of non-Muslims in the context of the call for Sharī'a from a cross-section of Muslims. Are non-Muslim minorities marginalized in this situation by religion *per se*, or are there other factors such as ethnicity, economics or sheer ignorance that hinder the promotion of the principles of Islamization? I will address these questions from my own background as a Muslim, an African and a woman; my examples will be taken from my own country, Ghana, as well as other places such as Nigeria and Sudan where Islamization has taken place. First, though, I wish briefly to set out the conceptual framework with which I shall be working.

Conceptual framework

My understanding of Islam is that it is an 'ecumenical' summons to the whole of creation to share in God's peace. According to the Qur'an, Islam is all-embracing in terms of nature, humankind and human history. Its mission is to proclaim this ecumenical understanding, which means to affirm Islam as the inherent or innate truth of all religions, and to challenge any religious pretensions which seek to limit the universality of divine revelation. This affirmation and challenge must be given by Muslims in relation to all other historical religions, but, at the same time they must apply with equal vigour to their own critique of historical Islam. Hence the Qur'an calls people of religion to an inter-religious dialectic. In particular, Muslims and Christians are called to engage in ecumenical dialogue in witness to the faith in God which they have in common, so that they can work together in fulfilling their mutual responsibility of seeking peace on earth through obedience to the divine will. The desire for community – a community of harmony and peace – is common to both Islam and Christianity.

Muslims and Christians are therefore called to action to establish the *umma* or the 'kingdom of God on earth'. They have a common agenda, which is not simply a matter of acknowledging one another's commonalities. The critical question is how Muslims and Christians can together establish the peace, justice and righteousness that underlie their traditions in contexts where, on the one hand, there is a constant cry for the application of the Sharī'a in Muslim communities with Christian minorities, and, on the other hand, Christians insist that their rights will be violated. Can Islamization be effected in the multi-religious and secular societies in which we live, in ways that will be meaningful and generally acceptable?

Setting the agenda

In a pluralistic society, questions of inter-communal harmony assume great importance. Freedom of conscience, speech and religion, and the right to profess as well as to propagate one's religious convictions consistently with law and morality will be regarded as inviolable rights of everyone in the modern world. Whilst contemporary discussion around the Muslim world regarding a more authentic way of life makes the question of Islamization a relevant topic on one hand, non-Muslims living in Muslim societies see this issue not merely as relevant but as threatening their very existence on the other. Islamization appears to have a stigma attached to it, and non-Muslims are very apprehensive about the whole process. It has been construed as militant, archaic and retrogressive, with very little to offer to the world, and as exhibiting a basic attitude of rejection towards those who do not belong to it.

This has come about as a result of the methodology adopted by those who wish to show their zeal for Islam and, who in their bid to demonstrate this, emphasize only the *hudūd* in a discriminatory way. As a Muslim, I too feel threatened by this militant way of doing things; it is also gendered. A further problematic area is the negative connotation associated with the classically formulated concept of the *dhimmī*, or non-Muslim living under the jurisdiction and protection of Islam. The arguments here hinge on the fact that the *dhimmī* is basically discriminated against, not being considered a full citizen. There arises therefore a polarity between Muslims and non-Muslims on the question of the status of the *dhimmī*.

Thus, using Islam as an ideology raises problems for the non-Muslim who does not believe in Islam. Islamization is perceived by non-Muslims as having different standards and laws for different sections of the population in the same state in matters of public concern. It would appear that with Islamization one religion is the axis around which public life revolves, and non-Muslims therefore cannot participate fully in the conduct of national life. This attitude not only frustrates the minority community, but also prevents its members from utilizing their capabilities to the fullest. In the long run, it may also deprive the state of some of its finest human resources.

While the general attitude of the media towards Sharī'a may be regarded as to some degree biased and prejudiced, and also as perpetuating stereotypes, certain approaches to Islamization and the status of non-Muslims have certainly given cause for alarm and reservation. Muslim attitudes have not helped the situation in several cases – for example in Nigeria, where the application of Islamization seems to be more interested in flogging (especially of women) rather than in creating wealth. This interpretation and application of the Sharī'a is stacked against women. It is not surprising that, for instance, during Numeiri's Islamization process in the Sudan, the Republican Brothers contended that the traditional interpretation of the Sharī'a, especially as it related to Muslim women and to non-Muslims, was outrightly discriminatory. Thus *fiqh* and its teachings on non-Muslims should be seen in its proper context. Verses relating to the *ahl al-kitāb* and the question of *dhimmī* status must be studied critically, analysed and evaluated in historical contexts.

As a Muslim who believes that Muslims should be able to live according to the principles of Sharī'a, the problem for me is not how to dissuade fellow Muslims. Rather, the problem is to see how Muslims can be objective and realistic in dealing with those who do not subscribe to their ideology yet who are a part of the same community. A related question is that of creating a congenial atmosphere of justice and freedom for Muslims themselves. Contemporary Muslims should not address these issues from the point of view of the classical formulations of *fiqh* if they are to minimize the fears and apprehensions held by non-Muslims. The question relating to the *jizya*, the concept of *dhimmī*, and the penalty for the apostate are typical examples which have to be explained contextually to be meaningful in the contemporary world.

As has been intimated, approaches to these issues from Muslims themselves have influenced some negative attitudes. Yet the Sharī'a as a system should not be seen as an instrument of oppression; properly interpreted and applied, it acknowledges and caters for the rights of non-Muslims. The Sharī'a has principles that can help improve the socio-economic, mental, emotional, and spiritual life of the human being, if applied properly. A Christian or a Muslim should not feel apprehensive about such a holistic system, because Christianity presumably stands for the same objective. This being so, there is need for a dialogue between the different religious traditions to map out a strategy in the contemporary world to achieve these goals.

In setting the agenda for any meaningful discussions between Christians and Muslims, it is also imperative to review the 'why' of Islamization in the contemporary world, especially as this is intricately related to extremism, a search for a voice, and a search for justice. I have often asked myself why I, as an African, should be subjected to British law and why I should be bound by it. Can I, as a matter of divine or human right, choose to revert to another system? Should not Africans, both Christians and Muslims, be able in principle to revert to traditional religions if they so wish, since that which the colonial systems have bequeathed to them is so alien to their culture? The history of colonialism and imperialism, and the legacy these have left for Africa, are well known, as are Africa's problems of poverty, disease and instability, and its struggles to become politically, economically and ideologically independent.

Marginalization and extremism

It is against this background that the agitations in various parts of the Muslim world can be considered – not with the intention of revisiting history and the pains associated with it, but rather to show that some policies have had, and continue to have, far-reaching implications and ramifications for Christian–Muslim relations. For example, colonial policy on education in Northern Ghana was such that Muslims were marginalized as a result of missionaries being asked not to operate schools in predominantly Muslim areas; in places where they did open schools, conversions took place. Thus, lack of education relegated Muslims to the periphery of the periphery. While this policy had nothing essentially to do with Christianity or with the teachings of Jesus, Muslims still view this marginalization in the light of religion as the implementers of the policy were Christians.

A critical question which must be addressed is this: what do people do when, as a result of perceived injustice and human rights violations, fundamentalists are pushed to the wall? How do displaced people react when the whole world does very little about their plight? For some people the answer lies in extremism. I do not subscribe to, and would not justify, such a reaction, yet it does seem that extremism is sometimes rooted in discontent, dissatisfaction, oppression and dejection. Therefore the fundamental human question of justice needs to be addressed, since it lies at the core of religion.

One way Muslim communities can seriously curb fundamentalism and extremism is for the authorities to give them a voice and constantly to engage in dialogue with them on critical issues. Through such a relationship, the authorities may come to appreciate some of the concerns raised by fundamentalists, and find ways of dealing with them before they get out of hand. Another way of trying to curb this tendency is for different Muslim organizations to meet regularly and deliberate on how to forestall these tendencies in their respective countries. Most importantly, in Muslim-dominated areas where there are minorities, special efforts should be made to contact, to engage in dialogue, and to find solutions to the needs of these minorities. Efforts should also be made to explain the Islamic religion to them in an intelligible manner, so that the minorities earn the trust of Muslims.

Education of the general Muslim community is critical in controlling the fundamentalist trend. This means that an academic study of religions in Muslim communities should pervade the educational system. In the same vein, Islam should be studied analytically and critically at all levels of society, whether formally or informally. Part of the curricula or syllabuses of educational institutions should address the question of how the Sharī'a can be made intelligible and meaningful in a modern democratic state. It should also emphasize peace studies, trying to inculcate values of love, tolerance and forgiveness through the family system. This would help in the moulding of progressive Muslims, true to their faith and also open-minded and tolerant. In dealing with the question of fundamentalism or extremism, it is also important to point out that, because Islam is in no way monolithic and there are divisions based on sectarian and spiritual lines, there can be no single model to emulate. This is in itself problematic, yet the question of extremism has to be tackled through education, which is a slow process. The Muslim academic community, therefore, has a major task ahead in taking up this challenge.

Contextualization

For me in Africa, setting the agenda also means dealing with bread and butter issues. Hence the discussions go beyond the academic discourse into other realms. Whilst issues of Sharī'a and *dhimmī* status may be of global relevance (and more so to us because of the Nigerian situation), Christians and Muslims already have an agenda given in Africa.

Despite the common global issues, this local context must also be given due consideration. A critical issue is how Muslims and Christians in Africa can work together to eradicate malaria, poverty, disease and corruption, and replace their society with peace and justice on the continent – the mosquito does not discriminate on the basis of religion.

The difficult economic situation of most African countries is well known. The insecurities in so many people's lives as a result of wars, famines and natural disasters make it imperative for Muslims to use resources within Islam to find solutions to such enormous problems. This could be achieved more effectively if people of faith were to mobilize resources to improve their social economic status, a step necessary to restore confidence and raise standards of living. It is a sin for a Christian to enquire about the religious affiliation of people before putting up a school in a particular area. In the same vein, it is un-Islamic, almost tantamount to *kufr* (ungratefulness), for a Muslim to build a well and not to make it accessible to non-Muslims. This contradicts the concept of social justice, which does not know of any distinction of Muslims and non-Muslims. Through the mercy and grace of God, even those who do not believe in God still enjoy his sustenance and his bounty.

A presupposition of such cooperation is that Muslims, Christians and all people should be alert to the political domain. It is the duty of all to criticize governments in Africa which are oppressive, dictatorial and unable to serve people. Muslims and Christians committed to creating the kingdom of God have much to do to create better, healthy and strong independent nations. In view of this, Muslims and Christians must do advocacy on these critical questions, most of which are not necessarily theological or religious. Muslims and Christians must collaborate and network in promoting peace and justice.

I have tried to show how these two religions are bonded on the basis of a common humanity with an agenda for action. There is a divine imperative not only to talk but to act. If this divine imperative must be successful, then on one hand Muslims must revisit the question of the *dhimmī* in the context of Islamic political reassertion. On the other hand, Christians must also appreciate the cultural and identity crises which Muslims are going through, and their effort to find an alternative lifestyle. Critical questions of the causes of extremism and fundamentalism need to be taken seriously, not glossed over as trivial issues. Although there are important global questions to discuss, contextualization of these issues in particular situations is indispensable.

Dialogue between Christians and Muslims today

Tarek Mitri

Agendas for dialogue

It may not be superfluous to start with a word of caution and critical assessment of what has been achieved, or attempted, in recent Christian–Muslim dialogue initiatives. We need to warn, but also immunize ourselves, against the contamination of such initiatives by the culture of suspicion. More often than not, Muslims are asked, not always in a subtle way, to distance themselves from those who have perpetrated indiscriminate acts of violence claiming to defend Islam and Muslims. Muslims are invited, sometimes in an unfriendly manner, to prove their innocence and that of their religion from the crimes committed by a minority of their co-religionists.

In many dialogue initiatives of the last few months, it is noticeable that suspicion has accentuated the temptations of globalism, essentialism and culturalism.

It is has become difficult to discard the resonating effects in many parts of the world of a discourse on the global confrontation between Christianity – or the West – and Islam. In short, misinterpreting or exaggerating the role of religions in the relations among and within nations marks attitudes and perceptions of various local tensions or conflicts, leading to their aggravation. Local relations between Muslims and Christians are significantly affected by the propagation of a globalist discourse.

Historically specific or culturally, politically and religiously diverse, the situations of Muslims in relation to non-Muslims remain, in the eyes of many, essentially the same. Many do not seem to be willing or able to recognize plurality, avoid precipitated comparisons and refrain from amalgamation. At best, the search for intellectual rectitude is dismissed as luxury.

For their part, a mix of advocates of secular or Christian cultural supremacy and liberal proponents of the respect for other cultures emphasize the distinctiveness of what is labelled as 'Islamic culture'. However, their exaggeration of the status of culture and its role in explaining personal and collective behaviour is less perceptible when they reflect on their own situations. Culturalists do not see the world except in terms of never-ending difference. In previous times, Western secularists, not only historians and sociologists of religion, searched for an essence of things religious common to all. In emphasizing similarities between religions they tried to discredit the Christian claim to uniqueness. Today, the emphasis of many, anthropologists and others, is on difference.

These considerations, if seen also from the perspective of the last thirty years of practical experience in Christian–Muslim dialogue, confirm the importance of 'setting the agenda' together. Christians and Muslims were often invited to take part in reflecting and acting on an agenda set unilaterally, largely by Christian partners, but also at times, by Muslims. Whenever it was desirable or possible to set the agenda in a common effort, dialogue was conducted on the basis of a minimalist or parallelist assumption. In both cases, divisive issues, both within religious communities and between them, were largely avoided.

The attempt to set a common agenda owned by Muslims and Christians is not meant to suggest that statements such as 'there will be no peace among nations unless there is peace among religions' and 'wars in the name of religion are wars against religions' are irrelevant, but rather to articulate together a few important questions, not shying away from the thorny issues of our time. These questions need to be formulated in a manner that facilitates speaking, at the same time, together and to each other.

Mutual learning

For years, the importance of mutual learning was affirmed. In the process of thinking through their approach to Islam, many Christians accepted that much of what has passed for 'objective scholarship' was not free of ideological bias.

Those who committed themselves to dialogue saw the beginning of a new understanding based on a reciprocal willingness to listen. They also became aware of the requirement to be willing to question one's own self-understanding and to be open to understand others in their own terms. A number of churches, theological faculties and other educational institutions have taken the initiative of promoting knowledge of Islam and Muslims. A number of similar efforts have recently been undertaken in some Muslim institutions. These have not developed without shortcomings and difficulties. Some of them arise from the limits and ambiguities of educating Christians about Islam by informed fellow Christians, somehow on behalf of Muslims. Others relate to the possibilities and challenge of inviting Muslims to educate Christians about Islam in a way that speaks to them and does justice to the plurality of ideas and approaches within the Islamic community.

Today, it is not uncommon to hear decision-makers, specialists or self-appointed specialists, journalists and others articulate a simple – and even simplistic – discourse, risking generalizations or surrendering to political expediency. It may be necessary to remind ourselves, in the context of education or public information, of the costly obligations of intellectual rectitude, moral integrity and the concern for communicability. We are faced with a patient, but urgent, task of learning about each other, interpreting one's own tradition as well as each other's. Christians who know Islam and Muslims who know Christianity, through scholarship and dialogue, need to work, not only on behalf of each other as the opportunities arise, but with each other.

Redressing media images and rectifying perceptions are, to be sure, the fruits of dialogue. At the same time, they make possible an authentic dialogue. In the present context, those who seek to hold in balance religious otherness and common humanity tread a narrow path. Globalized consumer culture works at reducing differences. Nationalist and communalist self-assertion tends to magnify them.

Religion, society and state

The way in which Christians and Muslims perceive each other's understanding of the relation between religion, society and state recurs significantly. With a varying measure of subtlety, many Christians depict Islam, and not just Islamism, as a call to theocracy. Parallel to that, many Muslims regard Christianity as a spiritual religion preoccupied with the life hereafter. In other words, the former attribute to Islam an amalgamation of political power and religious authority. They fail to recognize that while a separation between religion, society and state is not conceivable from an Islamic perspective, distinction between the realms of religion and politics is possible. The latter view Christianity as a religion that draws a radical separation between the two realms.

In general, Christians tend to assume that in Islam the state is not just an emanation of the community but is constitutive of it. Some of their Muslim counterparts associate secularism and contemporary Christianity. They point to the fact that Christianity in the West, after having defended theocratic state models, retreated, and later abdicated, before secularization. Moreover, in the course of their adjustment to the historical process that led to the privatization of religion, some Christians engaged in self-secularization and legitimated that theologically.

These mutual perceptions have been blurred further during the last few months. Today the assumption that we live in a secularized, and secularizing, world does not meet universal approval. To be sure, modernization has had great secularizing effects, more in some places than others. But it has also provoked powerful movements of counter-secularization. Certain religious institutions have lost power in many societies, but old and new religious beliefs and practices find their expressions, sometimes in an explosive manner. Conversely, religiously identified institutions play social and political roles even when fewer numbers of people believe or practise the religion that such institutions represent. In some extreme cases, people fight in the name of religions in which they have ceased to believe. There are conflicts between communities that have a religious past, but where their religious content is of no relevance. Religions in which people have little or no faith continue to define communities in which they have much faith.

It is therefore essential, when reflecting as Christians and Muslims on the role of religion in politics, international or national, to distinguish between political movements that may be genuinely inspired by religion and those that use religion as a convenient legitimization for political agendas based on quite non-religious interests.

Religions and cultures

Dialogue on religion and politics is inseparable, in today's world, from that on religion and culture. The contemporary Western world has been largely self-defined as secular, and Muslims gradually perceived it as such. But the mounting tendency to emphasize its historical and cultural identity, and to portray it as Christian or Judeo-Christian, does not go unnoticed. Non-Western Christians can often be identified culturally with the West and sometimes, in spite of their affirmed cultural and religious difference, suspected of political allegiance to Western powers, even if they do not enjoy or expect any support from them. It may seem to matter much less than a few decades ago that many Christians were major actors in anti-colonial independence movements and continue to be strong critics of Western dominance.

In the Muslim world, ideological thought patterns represent the West as selfish, materialistic and dominating. In the West, the equivalent thought patterns perceive Islam as irrational, fanatical and expansionist. In the age of global communication and migration, these thought patterns, in the variety of their subtle and not-so-subtle expressions, foster antagonism.

It is true that the issue of Islam and the West is more complex and more contingent upon contemporary concerns than either proponents or opponents of culturalist politics would imply. Many of the problems, such as foreign hegemony and intervention, terrorism and international threats, are confused and exaggerated. But they have become real issues although they are, in the main, relating to power of states, the treatment of migrant and minority groups and the balance of forces within many developing societies.

But it is not less true that the end of world-wide ideological confrontations, and the globalization of Islam, has favoured the re-emergence of perceptions where Islam and the West exist as subjective, imaginary constructs, which influence the way each sees the other. This is exacerbated by a paradox of globalization. The development of consumerism and planetary televised entertainment has produced unprecedented cultural homogenization and uniformity. But the more individuals, and peoples, look alike the more they need to affirm their differences. In many societies, people face the perspective of allying the 'worst of two worlds': a culturally homogeneous world and one where seeking identity and community goes the way of hostility towards the other.

Co-citizenship and human rights

The principles of co-citizenship, equality, the rule of law and human rights have been in the heart of the 'dialogue of life' between Christians and Muslims. Their universality was often affirmed, not withstanding differences in approaches and emphasis. In many situations, the cooperation of Christians and Muslims in upholding together these values gave significance to dialogue and put its credibility to the test.

Today, these issues need to be addressed, theoretically and practically, with renewed vigour and all over the world. The idea of co-citizenship deserves to be reaffirmed as the basis for genuine dialogue and cooperation between Christians and Muslims. Co-citizenship is the encounter of persons as equal actors in society and polity who, while influenced by culture, religion and ethnicity, cannot be reduced to the roles assigned to them in the name of communal identities, loyalties and perceived interests.

In a dialogue of co-citizenship, Christians and Muslims become aware that human rights should not be implemented selectively, instrumentalized in the context of external domination, or used by one group of people against another. For people of faith, it is crucial to affirm the indivisibility of human rights, to reconcile individual rights with those of communities, and to stand by victims whatever their ethnic or religious identity.

Thus, human rights advocacy should not be conditioned by confessional solidarity, no matter how legitimate. In this vein, the call for 'reciprocity' in the treatment of minorities is problematic. The logic of reciprocity, borrowed by religious communities from states, favours a world-view opposing an Islamic *umma* with Christendom, both imagined, each having a ramification in the 'abode' of the other. In their great diversity, minorities can unfortunately be perceived as victims or hostages, rather than as actors.

On a more specific note, many of the interests of Christian minorities cannot be safeguarded and promoted except in conjunction with those of the Muslim majorities among whom they live. Upholding the rights of Christians in the Muslim world, in a way that is seen as a form of foreign intervention pretexting their protection, reinforces the perception that they are aliens in their own countries or disloyal to them. Defending the rights of Christians in opposition to their Muslim co-citizens and neighbours, with whom they share culture and national identity, may aggravate the suspicion of majorities towards minorities, who can be seen as an instrument of a real or potential threat instigated by powerful forces.

The imperative of de-globalization

While relations between Muslims and Christians are strongly influenced by local and regional histories, they are increasingly impacted by world developments. It is mostly in situations where uncertainties of change begin to be felt that mistrust and mutual apprehension can build up between communities.

When communities are identified exclusively or even exaggeratedly by their religion, situations tend to become more explosive. Christianity and Islam carry, in region-specific ways, deep historical memories. They may appeal to universal loyalties that can be seen, in certain societies, as a cause of tension or conflict. But quite often they are not more than an intensifying feature of disputes whose main causes are outside religion.

There are cases where a conflict in one place, with its local causes and character, is perceived and instrumentalized as part of a conflict in another. So enmities in one part of the world spill over into situations of tension in other regions. An act of violence in one place is used to confirm stereotypes of the 'enemy' in another place, or even to provoke revenge attacks elsewhere in the world. It is not uncommon to see people, unable or unwilling to fight those who caused their anger, look for substitutes and easily find them. What is otherwise a remote conflict becomes a local problem. Neighbours hold each other accountable for the wrongs attributed to their co-religionists elsewhere. Unless they are prepared to dissociate themselves publicly from those with whom they share a common faith, they are accused of complicity with them.

It is therefore crucial to offer a prospect of counteracting the processes which tend to globalize conflicts that involve Muslims and Christians. In other words, it is necessary to 'de-globalize Christian–Muslim tensions' as a vital step towards resolving them. Attention to the specific local causes of conflicts helps to identify solutions to be found, first and foremost, in addressing those local causes. This is not possible unless the leaders of both communities refuse to be drawn into others' conflicts on the basis of uncritical response to calls for solidarity among adherents to one faith. It is only in applying common principles of peace, justice and reconciliation that parties to local conflicts are helped to release Islam and Christianity from the burden of sectional interests and self-serving interpretations of beliefs and convictions. Christian and Islamic beliefs and convictions can then constitute a basis for critical engagement with human weakness and defective social and economic orders in a common search for human well-being, dignity, social justice and civil peace.

Religions and violence

The problem of violence and its legitimation in religious thought and in the practice of religious communities has been discussed, episodically and often indirectly, in Christian–Muslim dialogue. In the eyes of some Christians, it was too divisive an issue to be dealt with in what continued to be a fragile process of building trust and mutual understanding. Implicitly, and sometimes explicitly, the divergence between Christian and Muslim positions was overstated. Today, the relationship between violence and religion is the object of a renewed attention, directed primarily at the Muslim approach to the problem. In some circles, there seems to be an impatient tendency to look for an explanation of the recent criminal attacks in the scriptural and canonical foundation or justification of violence. Thus, the non-religious factors determining symbolic and historical violence are not adequately examined, let alone exhausted, before addressing the religious dimension. The 'anatomy' of terrorism is privileged over its 'genealogy'. When some people hold traditional religious education responsible for spreading a culture of hatred, they fail to see that it is not the traditional religious values that lead people to violence but their loss, without much in counterpart, which explains frustration, grievance and revulsion. Violence cannot be explained by ancestral hatred, for ancestral hatred is reinvented and even fabricated as a result of violence.

It is only after examining the root causes of violence in their present reality as well as in their respective histories that Christians and Muslims can credibly reflect together, and share each other's internal discussions, on issues like *jihād*, just war and martyrdom. Thus, dialogue on violence will not be caught in criticizing, on one hand, the theological inconsistency of those who consider violence to be legitimate as defensive or as a last resort and, on the other hand, dismissing the pacifist utopia of those who choose to overcome violence through non-violence.

It remains true that the challenge before Christians and Muslims goes beyond these considerations. They need to learn from each other and discover, in local situations and at the world level, ways of holding together, without illusions but not without tensions, striving against injustice and making peace.

Looking forward together

Michael Nazir-Ali

Meeting together

The Lambeth seminar took place in the context of a rapidly changing and shrinking world. As the Prime Minister has pointed out, this can be for good or ill. If it is to be for a peaceful world order in which there is justice and compassion, it is necessary to begin to identify those principles and values which can help Christians and Muslims live together. From different parts of the world, seminar participants affirmed the importance of face-to-face encounter, not in a spirit of confrontation, but with a view to engagement of minds and hearts and with an exchange of information about themselves and the societies in which they live, so that what is common may be recognized and differences understood.

There was a consciousness that both faiths are universal, not only in intention, but, increasingly, in terms of geography, culture and ethnicity. This is, at least partly, because both understand themselves as having a missionary mandate. Both are also committed to the 'definitiveness' of their own revelation but, at the same time, allow reason to interact with revelation. This has serious implications for understanding revelation in terms of changing knowledge and new cultural contexts. In the end, both faiths are committed to seeking a dynamic consonance of reason and revelation.

In different ways, both faiths see human beings as stewards of God in the context of creation as a whole and in terms of human society. Whether it is the *kerygma* or proclamation of God's presence and work in Jesus Christ or the Islamic *balāgh* (or preaching), both have to be worked out in terms of social structures and systems. Ideas about citizenship and the values needed for the common good may have different origins but some, at least, are convergent, and this means that Christians and Muslims can work for social cohesion and international understanding, rather than being resigned to an inevitable 'clash of civilizations'.

Living together as Muslims and Christians?

Christians and Muslims have a very long history of living together. From the earliest days, when the Muslims, fleeing persecution, found refuge in Christian Abyssinia, through the explicit recognition of Christians and Jews in the constitution of Medina and the emergence of the *dhimma* in lands conquered by Muslims, down to our own times, people belonging to the two faiths have shared life together. Muslims have often provided conditions for the emergence of civilizations where Christians and others have been able to make a notable contribution to learning, administration and trade. In our own days, such living together has extended beyond Western Asia, Africa and parts of Europe to other parts of the world. For Muslims who find themselves in a minority, the challenge is to make sense of such a situation and to contribute to it becoming *dār al-sulh* (or place of reconciliation and peace). Where Christians are in a minority, there may be a need to move beyond a *dhimmī* mentality and to see themselves as not merely a tolerated and protected people but as full citizens with equal freedom of expression, belief and worship.

A plural context

Muslims and Christians do not find themselves engaged with one another in isolation but precisely in the context of a plural world with many religions, ideologies and world-views jostling each other and even competing for a hearing. This plurality has to be recognized as providing a proper context for Christian–Muslim relationships. Such a context also raises questions about how the scriptures of each faith are to be understood and received in the light of new knowledge; scientific, social and even religious. Convergent values, for Muslims and Christians, in the light of similar beliefs, have to be compared and brought to terms with values emerging from other, very different, ways of seeing the world and the human condition. A dynamic view of truth is needed in such a situation. Not only is truth given in a person or a book, but it is this truth itself which leads believers to the fullest revelation of itself.

Building civil society

Both Muslims and Christians must argue for the importance of religious guidance for the building of civil society. This cannot, however, be a case for theocracy. Religions will seek to inspire and to guide rather than to coerce. Christians will welcome much of the understanding of Sharī'a set out in the Muslim contributions here. It is a reminder that the Sharī'a is not to be understood as a series of legal, religious, social and penal prescriptions but as a way of remaining faithful in the totality of life. Christians can recall here that one of the earliest names for them was 'those of the Way'.[1] The necessity of *ijtihād* for the identification of what is basic and the distinguishing of essential principles from their cultural and temporal expression has been pointed out, and this can only contribute towards greater confidence between Muslims and Christians in every part of the world. It appears that, in both Sunni and in Shi'a Islam, there are principles of movement, as far as law is concerned, and this can allow a socially dynamic situation to emerge.

While the value of diversity has been acknowledged, it has also been recognized that this cannot be sheer diversity. It is controlled not only by the nature of the revealed texts themselves but also by the requirements of the individual and the common good.

Both religions have well-developed *mystical traditions* and these point to the true worth of inwardness; of a personal experience of the divine, of the importance of vocation as a believer, and of the need to develop an informed conscience which can guide action.

There are fundamental differences of belief and of approach between Christians and Muslims, but this dialogue shows that there are exciting possibilities for greater understanding and cooperation across a range of issues. This should not be the end of the matter but the beginning of finding new ways of learning and acting together.

Continuing on the journey

Should Muslims and Christians work jointly on matters like citizenship? There is a need to hear more about the ways in which thinking about development in Islamic law is actually affecting the legal situation in different countries. There is a need for further work in both the West and in Islamic countries on the question of discrimination on grounds of religion. How do Islam and Christianity understand human responsibilities and rights? How does this relate to international and national Human Rights legislation? Have the two faiths anything distinctive to say – and can they say at least some of this together?

At the seminar, we took a significant step in travelling together. The journey, however difficult it may prove to be, must continue for the sake of the world's future.

'And they returned by another route'

Gillian Stamp

Appreciative conversation

The work of the two-day seminar of 'building bridges' was hard, difficult and demanding. The medium was the presentation of papers and responses, some formal conversation, and a great deal of informal conversation. The tone was courage, grace, imagination and sensitivity in addressing and retreating from painful issues.

The demand came from the hard work of listening and remaining serene whilst hearing views and ideas that could disturb, even distress. That kind of listening is possible only when people do all they can to suspend their desire to judge, to control, to change the other person. This 'appreciative conversation' of listening with openness and mutual respect is especially important at the moment when many world influences and events predispose to fragmentation, polarization and stalemate.

The hallmark of an 'appreciative conversation' is that people listen without judgement, do not seek consensus or compromise, but share the sole purpose of continuing the conversation in order to sustain relationships of mutual respect. This requires generosity of spirit and discipline, and both were clearly present. There were also difficulties – voices present not heard, or silenced, or heard through filters; and inevitably, many unheard voices from the communities that form the hinterland of the gathering. There seemed to be an imbalance in questions – 'the questions are all about Islam, the face of Christianity is covered'. But the overall sense was of the work of an appreciative conversation in which each person remained rooted in his or her background whilst at the same time reaching beyond it.

The four journeys

The journey is an image in all faiths carrying the sense of companionship and a future. In the course of a journey people live, work and think together and there is likely to be at least the tentative emergence of a common mind, a common spirit, as well as common work. The idea of a shared future (denied by tendencies to fragmentation, polarization and stalemate) is a given. Leadership for the well-being of people in that future depends on making decisions now that do not close off options for the leaders yet to come.

There was the profound change of being and working together distilled in the lines of T. S. Eliot about the magi who 'returned by a different route':

> We returned to our places, these Kingdoms,
> But no longer at ease here, in the old dispensation.[2]

It may be helpful to think about the work of the gathering as four distinct and interwoven journeys: the historical, the public, the private and the reflective. This framework can as well be used to think about individual lives – what unfolds as time passes, life at work, life at home and the life of reflection.

The historical journey

The work done to understand and appreciate the history of the two faiths was acknowledged, as was the urgent need for acceptance that there are conflicting narratives of events and of ideas and a need to be aware of the fallacy of like-mindedness. Thought was given to seeing the history of Europe as that of both faiths, as the background to facing contemporary challenges of secularism, materialism, and economic inequalities. And to the very different situations in different settings across the world – with legacies of colonialism and expansion. The appreciation of this background is part of the clearly expressed need to separate religion from culture and to understand that in Muslim ontology there can be no separation between the sacred and the secular, although many – like Christians – now live in cultures where that division is a given. This gives particular poignancy to the individual task of being faithful to religion and facing the society in which the person is living and working.

One of the painful areas in this historical journey is the view that there is in some way a single path of 'progress' that Christianity has trodden and that Islam will follow. The ways in which deeply held and very different views about this were discussed, addressed and retreated from was one clear example of the work and the value of 'appreciative conversation'. As Martin Buber put it: 'If we go on our way and meet a man [sic] who has advanced towards us and has also gone on *his* way, we know only our part of the way, not his – his we experience only in the meeting.'[3]

So this first journey was well covered – both in the seminar and in earlier gatherings and writings – but not without pain and the care that required.

The public journey

This was the working and thinking together of the formal sessions – the papers, the responses and the conversations that followed. For each faith and each individual there is another public journey – in communities, regions, globally. The essence of this journey is that it is public with all that means in what is said, what commitments are made, what is achieved, what others perceive. It is this work that the 'hinterland' of hope and meaning and also unease and suspicion will see, respond to, criticize, feel involved in, excluded from, heard, not heard.

The advantage of the formality of the design of this public journey is that it was possible for delicate matters to be spoken of. The disadvantage is that time constraints meant it was not possible to have the less formal conversations that could have taken matters forward. The groundwork has been laid and time can be arranged differently for future gatherings.

The public journey enters directly a world where human interconnectedness is stretched to – perhaps beyond – its limits. The context is of globalization – of information, investment flows, and impacts of events. And of inequality, homogenization of culture especially through television and mobile technology, of different demographic pressures – young, disenfranchised people in some parts of the world, ageing populations facing anxiety about their old age in others. And both faiths face the challenges of secularism, materialism, metropolitan cities and the postmodern philosophies that spring from them.

In this seminar, the geo-political and economic context was mentioned but not built directly into papers or discussion. The public journeys of both faiths would be strengthened if more time were given to it. This would make it possible to think together about how to engage with and influence its local and global impacts. And thus to take steps to translate the shared thinking of leaders into the daily lives of people and vice versa. Wider appreciation of the global context would also make it possible to communicate a more multi-faceted picture of both Islam and Christianity.

As the public journey – of this gathering and of each faith and individual leader – moves on, one of its first responsibilities is to think about and act on ways to connect with and receive from people at the 'grass roots'. This could be significant in those communities where people of one faith are a minority. It will also be important to engage those not already engaged. And not only 'to discuss those things our communities would like us to be discussing' but also to have the courage and face the hurt and criticism of talking about matters communities might not want to have discussed.

It is inevitable that leaders and thinkers will work towards common ground that is different – and can appear very distant – from the concerns and commonalities of peoples' daily lives. A key responsibility of leaders is to translate from one to the other, cultivating 'growing edge' people and accepting the censure of those who are far from that edge and not yet ready to see it. In this way they minimize the risk of making statements about common values which are not connected with the choices people make each day about how they will behave at work, towards their neighbours, in their worship.

The private journey

This was the journey – the work of conversation – that took place in the breaks. It was the base for the 'joint collegiality', the growth of mutual understanding and respect between people, some of whom knew each other, many who did not. Initial wariness moved on to quieter, stiller listening, to gentle venturing into sensitive areas, to warmer less detached interest in different beliefs. Values could be seen as less 'exotic'; less a matter of curiosity, more one of respect.

As with the individual, so with this gathering, the private is a source of sustenance for the public journey. As with us all, the public can so easily take precedence – of time, energy, attention – over the private. It may be helpful to make space for small groups where stories can be told and heard. Rumi distils the deep value of stories in his poem 'Story Water':

> A story is like water
> that you heat for your bath.
>
> It takes messages between the fire
> and your skin. It lets them meet,
> and it cleans you!
>
> Very few can sit down
> in the middle of the fire itself
> like a salamander or Abraham.
> We need intermediaries . . .
>
> Water, stories, the body,
> all the things we do, are mediums
> that hide and show what's hidden.
>
> Study them,
> and enjoy this being washed
> with a secret we sometimes know,
> and then not.[4]

The reflective journey

Like the image of the journey, reflection is of the essence of both faiths in that it makes possible a more attentive way of life – to do anything reflectively is to nurture the connection with a deeper self. This journey pauses, considers, tends the other journeys and holds them together when, as so easily happens, they slip apart.

Part of the work of this journey is to sustain the listening of appreciative conversation. This kind of listening is an attitude towards another person(s) that begins with attention and communicates attentiveness. It is demanding because each of us knows what it is to be ourselves in a way in which we know nothing else, and our natural inclination is to talk rather than to listen. Most of the time we narrow our attention so that it is like 'a questing beast, keeping its nose close down to the trail, running this way and that upon the scent, but blind to the wider surroundings'.[5] People and things are seen according to whether or not they serve particular purposes, and not for their own sake. Attentive listening depends on 'wide attention' that wants nothing other than understanding and has no agenda to change, judge or control the other. And this depends on knowing ourselves both as individuals and / or as a group. As the Prophet is reported to have said: 'He who knows himself, knows his Lord.'[6]

As the life of this dialogue continues, so the need for the work of this journey will increase. It is almost as if appreciative conversation emerged 'naturally' and was sustained for much of the time, although not without difficulty and some tensions. But it is fragile and in need of the continuous mindfulness, the continuous tending of the reflective journey.

Appreciative conversation is an important countervailing influence to the tendencies to polarization and stalemate inherent in the contemporary world. The reflective work needed to sustain it is thus of the essence.

Possible next stages of the journeys

1. Islam and Christianity both face the challenges of secularism. One way forward is for conversations in universities that include Muslim, Christian and secular scholars.

2. The dilemma of assimilation versus isolation, the work of being faithful to religion, of not denying the self and of facing the reality of the society in which one lives is experienced by both Muslims and Christians, and this could be a deep and productive theme to explore.

This lends itself readily to translating, bridging scholarly and personal experience and thinking, and so could be a way forward that would link the public journey to the 'minute particulars' of peoples' daily lives. It could be a strong base to reach out for and gather in experiences of daily reality – examples of hurt and confusion as well as living together and of active cooperation.

This would help to understand the conditions in which the latter is more likely to flourish and would make it easier for people of different faiths to live, work and even think together in the details of their everyday lives.

3. Talking together about conscience in interpretation of scripture. Both Islam and Christianity see human autonomy as a creation of God. The basic principle is permission, so there is potential for change – 'The Qur'an is outward revelation, the mind inward revelation.'

Whilst this view may not be held by all, it is a possible way forward to a shared understanding of the role of individual judgement.

Postscript
Ways ahead

Michael Ipgrave

Understanding one another

There is a need to deepen and to broaden the base of mutual understanding between Muslims and Christians. The academic community has a particular role to play in helping to counteract stereotypes, myths and facile generalizations. Educational institutions aligned with either faith, particularly those with a responsibility for training religious leaders, need to offer accurate, contemporary and authentic education about the other. In the first place, this needs to express the understanding that each community has of its faith from its own perspective. However, a rightful emphasis on self-understanding should not inhibit Muslims from moving on to the task of giving an Islamic evaluation of, and response to, Christianity, and likewise conversely for Christians. Christians and Muslims need to be honest with one another, and self-critical where this is called for. Only this attitude can give them sufficient confidence in one another to address sensitive and complex issues such as the relation between religions and violence or injustice.

Citizens together

Muslims and Christians need to explore intensively what it means to be citizens together of the world and of the various societies in which they live, with all their complexities and varieties. There needs to be agreement on shared universal values, and local and regional cooperation in applying these in particular contexts. Freedom of religion should be an imperative for both faiths, and majority religious leaders should have a particular concern for minorities in their societies. The rights of women need to be defined and defended, and special attention should be paid to the experiences and concerns of young people. Christians and Muslims should in all situations unite around the cause of justice, at global, regional, national and local levels, and form working partnerships for advocacy. Among specific issues of concern to Christians and Muslims, the Palestinian situation is bound to occupy a special place.

119

Broadening the circle

Dialogue and cooperation between Christians and Muslims should not be developed in an exclusive way. People and communities of other faiths hold many of the same concerns and values; there is much scope for fruitful interaction on a wider inter faith basis. Moreover, Jewish communities in particular share with Christians and Muslims in the Abrahamic heritage; trilateral initiatives flourish in several places, and should be encouraged wherever possible. Muslims and Christians need to find ways of addressing together the challenges and opportunities that are posed by the complex set of forces and situations known as secularism, and there is much here that either faith can learn from the other's experiences and attitudes.

Remembering God

Muslims and Christians should not be hesitant in speaking of God when they meet with one another. They both seek, in different ways, to witness to the reality of the one God in the world that he has made and sustains. Theological dialogue should not be avoided or made secondary to more apparently pressing social concerns, and it should have sufficient maturity to be able to address points of difference as well as areas of convergence. Christians and Muslims in their meeting need not only to speak of God but to be aware of his presence, adopting a generous and open attitude to each other's spiritual life and aspirations. When those who have faith in God meet with an open acknowledgement of their faith, the quality of their meeting is transformed, and together they can change the world.

Glossary

This glossary provides brief explanations of some of the technical terms appearing in the papers. Most of the entries below are Arabic (Ar.) words; others are English, French (Fr.), Greek (Gr.), Latin (La.), Malay (Ma.), Persian (Pe.), Spanish (Sp.) and Urdu (Ur.)

Adab (Ar.) The basic sense of 'good manners' covers a wide range of meanings: etiquette, culture, *belles-lettres*, etc.

Ahl al-kitāb (Ar.) 'People of the Book': those communities who, according to Islamic belief, have divinely revealed scriptures, particularly Jews and Christians, but also 'Sabians'. The *ahl al-kitāb* traditionally qualified as *dhimmī* (q.v.).

Akbar; akbariyya; Allāhu akbar (Ar.) Akbar means literally 'greater', i.e. 'greater than any other', 'most great', and therefore uniquely predicated of God. *Akbariyya* is the quality of being *akbar*; the *takbir* is the declaration of the surpassing greatness of God, *Allāhu akbar*.

A-lastu bi-rabbikum (Ar.) 'Am I not your Lord?': a question addressed by God to the children of Adam in Surah 7.172; their reply witnesses to the truth of his lordship.

Amāna (Ar.) The 'trust' offered by God to creation and to humanity, Surah 33.72.

Augustinianism Tradition of Western theology and philosophy tracing its inspiration to St Augustine of Hippo (354–430).

Balāgh (Ar.) Islamic 'preaching' or exhortation, specifically the message set forth by the Prophet in obedience to the divine command.

Christology Christian doctrine and theology relating to the person and work of Jesus Christ.

Commercium in spiritualibus (La.) 'Spiritual exchange': for example, the French Roman Catholic Islamicist Louis Massignon taught that Islam served to remind Christianity of the primacy of God, while Christianity provided a fulfilment of Islamic spirituality.

Convivencia (Sp.) The period of coexistence and cultural interaction between Muslims, Christians and Jews in Muslim-ruled Spain, particularly Andalusia, before the completion of the *reconquista* (q.v.).

Cuius regio eius religio (La.) 'In a [prince's] country, the [prince's] religion.' Principle that the ruler of a particular territory should be responsible for choosing the faith of all his or her subjects. The formula was agreed at the Peace of Augsburg (1555) as a way of settling the religious allegiance of the various territories of the Holy Roman Empire.

Dār al-sulh (Ar.) Literally 'house of treaty' (also *dār al-'ahd*); a territory which is neither under Islamic rule (*dār al-islām*) nor in opposition to Islam (*dār al-harb*, 'house of war'), but which enjoys treaty relations with an Islamic state.

Dawla (Ar.) State, specifically *dawla islamiyya*, 'Islamic State'.

Dhikr (Ar.) 'Remembrance' or 'recollection' of God: in Sufism particularly, through recitation of the divine names.

Dhimma; dhimmī (Ar.) System of protection of recognized minorities within traditionally organized Islamic societies (*dhimma*); member(s) of protected minorities (*dhimmī*). The system guaranteed freedom of worship and security from harassment, but imposed certain restrictions. It was generally available to the *ahl al-kitāb* (q.v.), who in return were required to pay a *jizya* or 'poll tax'.

Dīn 'Religion, piety': that which concerns the spiritual.

Ecumenical Council Assembly of bishops and other ecclesiastical representatives drawn from the world-wide Church whose decisions are considered binding on all Christians. Different branches of the Church differ as to the number of Ecumenical Councils recognized. Seven are generally accepted in East and West; the Roman Catholic Church holds that twenty-one ecclesiastical councils have ecumenical authority, the most recent being the Second Vatican Council (1962–65).

Fiqh; faqīh (Ar.) Islamic jurisprudence (*fiqh*); practitioner of jurisprudence (*faqīh*). Sunni fiqh recognizes major Schools of Law.

Gustakh-e-rasūl (Ur.) Legal provision concerning the offence of 'defiling the name of the Prophet Muhammad'. Section 295C of the Pakistani Penal Code.

Hadīth (Ar.) Tradition recording a saying or act of the Prophet Muhammad, attested by reliable authorities.

Hajj (Ar.) Islamic pilgrimage to Mecca.

Hakīm; hakeem (Ar.) A learned or wise person; a doctor (of medicine or philosophy).

Hijra (Ar.) The migration of the Prophet and other Muslims (the *muhājirūn*) from Mecca to Medina in 622. The Islamic calendar takes the *Hijra* as Year 1.

Huda (Ar.) Divine guidance.

Hudūd (Ar.) Literally 'limits' imposed by God: penalties for certain crimes which specified in the Qur'an or *hadīth*. The singular form is *hadd*.

'Idda (Ar.) Period of waiting which must be observed before a divorced woman is able to remarry.

'Īd al-adhā; 'Īd al-fitr (Ar.) Two principal feasts of the Islamic calendar. *'Īd al-adhā* is associated with the *hajj* pilgrimage to Mecca. *'Īd al-fitr* marks the end of the fasting month of *Ramadān*.

Ijtihād (Ar.) Jurisprudential term, literally 'exertion'. It indicates the development of new law to fit new situations, through the exercise of independent judgement reasoning from the sources where law is not self-evident.

Jihād (Ar.) 'Struggle' (in the cause of God). The word has a wide range of meanings, including the spiritual challenge to strive against sinful impulses, but is often used specifically to indicate armed conflict undertaken for Islam.

Jizya (Ar.) The poll-tax payable by the *dhimmī* (q.v.).

Kerygma (Gk.) Preaching specifically, the content of the apostolic proclamation of Jesus Christ as crucified and risen Lord.

Khilāfa (Ar.) 'Vice-gerency' or 'lieutenancy': used of the Qur'anic teaching that human beings are appointed by God as his 'representatives' (*khalīfa*) on earth. The concept broadly corresponds to the Christian idea of 'stewardship'.

Kufr (Ar.) 'Ungratefulness', with the further meaning of 'infidelity', and therefore 'unbelief' or 'atheism'.

Lavra (Gk.) Early form of monastic community, particularly in Palestine, consisting of a number of separate individual cells under the overall authority of a single abbot.

Lex credendi, lex orandi (La.) 'Law of believing' and 'law of praying'. The two are coordinated to indicate that a sure guide to what a Christian community believes is to be found through examining the forms it uses in prayer and worship.

Libido dominandi (La.) 'Lust to dominate': a phrase used by St Augustine to describe the sinful urge to oppress others, issuing from self-will, which he identified as lying at the root of the project to build the 'earthly city'.

Magisterium (La.) Central teaching authority within the Christian Church considered hierarchically, particularly the Papacy in the Roman Catholic Church.

Magnificat (La.) Christian expression of praise, from the Blessed Virgin Mary's exclamation 'My soul magnifies [i.e., proclaims the greatness of] the Lord', *Magnificat anima mea Dominum* (Luke 1.46).

Maqsad; maqāsid (Ar.) Goal or objective underlying a particular ordinance.

Mariolatry Excessive devotion to Mary the mother of Jesus. The charge of Mariolatry has sometimes been levelled by Muslims against Christians, and frequently by Protestants against Roman Catholics and Orthodox.

Melkite 'Imperial', i.e. dyophysite, Church – see next entry.

Monophysite 'One nature', i.e. believing that there was only one (divine) nature of the incarnate Christ. This was the belief held by those Churches of the East which refused to accept the *dyophysite* ('two natures', human and divine) definition of the Council of Chalcedon (AD 451). Relations between the Monophysites and the imperially authorized *Melkite* (dyophysite) Churches were very strained on the eve of the advent of Islam.

Nahda (Ar.) Renaissance or renewal of a culture or society.

Niyya (Ar.) Intention behind an action: an important jurisprudential factor in assessing any act.

Outre mer (Fr.) Literally 'beyond the sea': term used by medieval French to describe the Crusader kingdoms and principalities established in the Middle East, and by extension used of other European overseas ventures traceable in their inspiration to the Crusading movement.

Qibla (Ar.) Direction of Muslim prayer (*salāt*) towards Mecca, and so the orientation of a mosque.

Rasūl; risāla (Ar.) 'Messenger' (*rasūl*) entrusted with God's message (*risāla*) for the world. The word can be applied to any of the Prophets who brings a major new revelation, but is often used simply to indicate the Prophet Muhammad.

Reconquista (Sp.) The series of campaigns led by the Christian kingdoms of Northern Spain which eventually put an end to Muslim rule in the south of the country and to the tradition of *convivencia* (q.v.). The *reconquista* was completed with the capture of Granada by Ferdinand and Isabella in 1492.

Salāt (Ar.) Islamic canonical or ritual prayer, offered five times daily.

Al-Shaitan al-rajīm (Ar.) Literally, 'stoned Satan'. Satan, or *Iblīs*, 'the devil', is according to the Qur'an cast down by God for refusing to acknowledge Adam. The *hajj* pilgrimage includes a ritual of casting stones at a pillar in *Minā* (near Mecca), in memory of Abraham's rejection of Satan's temptations.

Sharī'a (Ar.); **'syariat** (Ma.) Islamic law, formulated according to the principles of *fiqh* from sources in the Qur'an and *Sunna*, and through the development of *ijtihād*. The broadest meaning of the word (as in Sadrach Surapranata's use of *syariat*) is to describe a divine path which should be followed.

Sīra (Ar.) Biography, particularly of the Prophet Muhammad.

Societas perfecta (La.) 'Perfect [in the sense of 'complete'] society.' A term used to describe the Roman Catholic Church in organizational terms, particularly prominent before the Second Vatican Council. It refers to the self-sufficiency and autonomy of the institutional Church, in this respect paralleling the sovereignty of the nation-state.

Sunna (Ar.) The tradition of the Prophet Muhammad, embracing his deeds and words (as recorded in the various *hadīth*). The *Sunna* is regarded by Muslims as second only to the Qur'an as a source of guidance.

Takbīr (Ar.) The declaration of God's greatness, *Allāhu akbar* (q.v.).

Tanzīl (Ar.) 'Revelation' (of the Qur'an).

Taqwā (Ar.) Piety, springing from the awe of God; 'fear of God'.

Thomism Tradition of Western theology and philosophy tracing its inspiration to St Thomas Aquinas (*c* 1225–1274).

Umma (Ar.) The community, people or nation of Islam worldwide.

Velayāt-e-fuqahā (Pe.) 'Rule of the jurists': political system where power is located in the those learned in Islamic law.

Zakāt (Ar.) Alms or tax obligatory on Muslims (one of the Five Pillars).

Notes

Chapter 1   Christians and Muslims face to face

1   Ps. 42.2.

2   Surah 2.115.

3   Paulo Coelho, *The Alchemist*.

4   Derived, respectively, from: *amir [al-bahr], al-jabr, al khuwārizmī, as-sumūt, kālib, al-kīmiya, kutun, khil'a, mahya, matrah, sūkkar, trafiq, sumut*, and *sifr*.

5   *Introductorium . . . astronomiae*, tr. Hispalensis (1135–53), ed. Venice: 1482–5, 1502–21.

6   *De motu stellarum* ('trigonometry'), tr. Plato of Tivoli (fl. 1140), ed. Nuremberg: 1537.

7   *Canonis Avicennae*, tr. Gerard de Cremona (1114–87), ed. Milan: 1473, Venice: 1523, Rome: 1593.

8   *De proprietatibus animalium*, tr. unknown, ed. Venice: 1497, 1500.

9   *De crepusculis*, tr. Gerard de Cremona (1114–87), ed. Lisbon: 1542.

10   *Flos naturarum*, tr. unknown, ed. Rome: 1473.

11   The Hakeem Man ('wise man') is derived from the notion of the *Bayt al-Hikmah* (the House of Wisdom) that was established in Baghdad (830 CE) by the Abbasid Caliph al-Ma'mun for the purpose of translation of Greek philosophy into Arabic language. See Susan L. Douglass and Karima Alavi, *The Emergence of Renaissance: Cultural Interactions Between Europeans and Muslims* (Fountain Valley, CA, USA: Council on Islamic Education, 1999), pp. 238–9.

12   Dzevad Karahasan, 'Islam, modernost i humanizam', *Oslobodenje* (Kun), 20/12/2001, pp. 2–3.

13   Surah 5.51.

14   George Schöpflin, *The New Politics of Europe: Nations, Identity, Power* (Hurst, 2000), p. 10.

15   *The Attitude of the Church towards the Followers of Other Religions: Reflections and Orientations on Dialogue and Mission* (Vatican Secretariat for Non-Christians, 1984). The Secretariat was subsequently renamed as the Pontifical Council for Inter-Religious Dialogue.

16   Declaration on Religious Liberty *Dignitatis Humanae* [1965], cap. 1, in Austin Flannery OP, ed., *Vatican Council II: The Conciliar and Post-Conciliar Documents* (Dominican Publications, 1975), p. 800.

17   Muhammad Arkoun, a North African thinker, in *Ouvertures sur l'Islam* (Paris, 1989). See also Jacques Waardenburg, 'Some North African Intellectuals' Presentation of Islam', in Y. Y. Haddad and W. Z. Haddad, eds, *Christian–Muslim Encounters* (Gainsville, 1995), pp. 358–80.

18   Surahs 17.110, 20.8.

19   Surah 17.111.

20   Surah 2.30.

21   *Niyya* is the Islamic term for the focus of 'intention' used to begin each of the 'Pillars of Religion' as truly deliberate and alert. A negligent approach would never be right.

22   'Anthropic' in that nature is seen as responsive to human intelligence and human intelligence minded towards nature's phenomena and meanings – or, as William Blake had it, 'cities and villages in the human bosom'. There is nothing 'arrogant' or hostile to inanimate nature in this perception, only a (hopefully) reverent realism.

23   There is – and needs to be – a rigorous distinction between 'the secular' (as argued here) and complete 'secularization', i.e. the exclusion of God. The 'faith-neutrality' of the 'secular' state might imply that religion is entirely an 'optional' privacy. But it need not do so and, in many cases, a historically 'primary' religious tradition will be in place, and may well remain dominant, so long as – on this view – it holds away from being 'domineering'. The 'secular' in this carefully defined sense is not only the actual situation of our volitional 'dominion'; it may also be greatly to the help of religious integrity in *not* conniving with the hypocrisies that go with enforced conformity (or the tribulations).

24   Echoing Surah 75.36: 'Does man think that he is left on the loose?' 'Tether' (roaming within limits) is fair imagery for the Qur'anic theme of 'bounds and limits' to be observed (*hudud*).

25   Iris Murdoch, *The Sovereignty of Good* (London, 1970), p. 79. It is important to realize that this 'atheism' does not make her 'value-free' or ethically adrift. On the contrary, her whole care is for a human *islam*, or fealty to the good as 'sovereign', but a 'good' finally under our control and of our devising. Prominent in her concept is the urge our selfhood shows to have the 'consolations of self-pity . . . fantasy and despair' she finds implicit in the lust for religious 'authority' (p. 91).

26   There are numerous passages that wonder at 'the embryo conceived and growing in the womb' to be launched into life – cf. Surahs 96.2, 30.21, 7.189, 4.21 and many others.

27   Rom. 5. 8.

28   Surah 17.111.

29   Surah 33.71.

30   'Pundit' comes to English from the Hindu *pandit*, meaning a sage well versed in Sanskrit lore. It now captures well the idea of being pretentious in a *magisterium*, as if truths had no better guardians than ourselves.

31   This would seem to be in line with the Sunni role of *ijmā'* (consensus) in the finalizing of religious law and principle. That most Muslims are the 'definers' of Islam cannot be in doubt. The question of which Muslims is always at stake, with 'experts' wanting to limit the necessary *ijtihād* or 'diligence' towards reaching *ijmā'* or 'closing the door' to it, as if all necessary had already been done. That does no justice to the ongoing issues of moving years or to the 'finality' of Islam as 'abreast of all futures'. When the newly created State of Pakistan debated its Constitution it wanted a 'Basic Principles Committee' to devise ways of scrutinizing all legislation, holding that a Muslim Legislature would not suffice for ensure Islamicity. But it invoked the

principle of 'non-repugnancy' to the Qur'an (a looser test than 'conformity to it'). This would seem to leave room for reference to the whole community of Muslims.

32   Kwame Nkrumah, *The Autobiography* (London, 1957), p. 164.

33   Surahs 5.99, 13.40, 24.53, 29.18, 36.17 and 42.48.

34   Surah 6.107.

35   Surah 10.100.

36   Surah 18.6.

37   See the case as made by 'Ali 'Abd al-Rāziq in *Islām wa Usul al-Hukm* ('Islam and the Sources of Jurisprudence', Cairo, 1925), in which, responding to the Turkish abolition of the Caliphate, he argued that it had never been integral to Islam and that its demise need in no way be deplored. Cf. the more recent writings of the eminent Cairo jurist Muhammad Said al-'Ashmawy – Arabic titles in English would be: Political Islam (1992), The Islamic Caliphate (1992) and The Essence of Islam (1992), all published in Cairo. The only 'caliphs' in the Qur'an are we humans exercising our given 'dominion' in Allah's Name. We are the *khulafā'* (pl.).

38   On the principle *cuius regio eius religio*, see 'Glossary'.

39   Even where non-Muslims are much fewer than in these named lands, they should be the more in line for solicitous care, being the more exposed.

40   If there is any analogy between how Zionist Jews see absence from the 'land' as precluding a true Jewishness and an Islamic insistence on 'the State' as indispensable to a true Islam, then Muslims living under what is not Islamic are in a similar 'exile' from a right condition. Having opted for diaspora, many see loyalty to their adopted home as a Muslim vocation. 'Subversive' ones, however, would see their duty as working for its overthrow. Cf. Zakaria Bashier, *The Hijrah: Story and Significance* (Leicester, 1983): 'Islam . . . lays clear and unambiguous claim to government . . . Non-Muslim societies will never accept, nor enable, a truly conscious Muslim – a Muslim who is fully aware of his full identity as Muslim – to realise the ideals of Islam.' He must 'challenge the sterile communities and cultures that refuse to heed the divine call of Islam' (pp. 103–5). He notes in passing that, when Muslims were stateless in Mecca, Arabic had no word for 'hypocrites' (*munafiqun*). It has been estimated that 'exilic' (i.e., diaspora) Muslims now number about one quarter of all the Muslims in the world – a very sizeable proportion.

41   John Donne, *Poetical Works* (ed. H. J. C. Grierson, Oxford, 1912), 'Third Satyre', vol. 1, p. 158, lines 100–102.

42   Gerard Manley Hopkins, *The Poems*, ed. W. H. Gardner and M. H. MacKenzie, 4th ed. (Oxford, 1970), p. 54 – being Stanza 10 in 'The Wreck of the Deutschland'.

Chapter 2   Learning from history

1   'Muslim–Christian interrelations historically: an interpretation', in W. C. Smith, *On Understanding Islam: Selected Studies*, Amsterdam, 1981, pp. 247–64.

2   Kwame Bediako, *Christianity in Africa: Renewal of a Non-Western Religion*, Edinburgh, 1995.

3   'Christian–Muslim relations in the twenty-first century', *Islamochristiana*, 24, 1998, p. 49.

4   M. Haykal, *The Life of Muhammad*, (tr. I. Al-Faruqi), North American Trust Publications, 1976, pp. 97–101.

5   Surah 5.82.

6   Al-Faruqi asks the intriguing question of whether this migration was devised 'merely for escape from injury, or . . . at least in the foresight of Muhammad, [for] a political motive that the historian ought to investigate and clarify'. (*The Life of Muhammad*, p. 100).

7   'Islam and the *Summa Theologica Arabica*, Rabi' 1, 264AH', *Jerusalem Studies in Arabic and Islam*, 13, 1990, p. 238.

8   Caspar, R. 'Les versions arabe du dialogue entre le Catholicos Timothee 1 et le Caliphe al-Mahdi', *Islamochristiana*, 3, 1977, pp. 107–75.

9   'Christianity in a pluralistic world: the economy of the Holy Spirit', *Ecumenical Review*, 1971, pp. 118–28.

10   Norman Daniel, *Islam and the West: The Making of an Image*, Edinburgh, 1960. The reference is to Dan. 7.23.

11   Shlomo Pines (tr.), University of Chicago Press, 1963.

12   *Islamic Spain: 1250–1500*, University of Chicago Press, 1990.

13   Gulnar Francis-Dehqani, *Religious Feminism in an Age of Empire: CMS women missionaries in Iran, 1869–1934*, Ph.D. Thesis, University of Bristol, 1999, pp. 111–12.

14   *Muslim Devotions: A Study of Prayer Manuals in Common Use*, London, 1961.

15   Sutarman Partonadi, *Sadrach's Community and Its Contextual Roots: A Nineteenth Century Javanese Expression of Christianity*, Amsterdam, 1990, p. 221.

16   This prophecy of the ultimate triumph of Islam occurs three times in the Qur'an – Surahs 9.33, 48.28 and 61.9. In the former, it is immediately followed by criticisms of Christian leaders.

17   On this section, cf. Tarif Khalidi, tr. and ed., *The Muslim Jesus: Sayings and Stories in Islamic Literature* (Harvard, 2001), passim.

18   As such, it had its origins as an option offered to conquered peoples on submission – the alternatives being either being killed or integration into Islam. The *jizya* was then the substitution of a financial offering in place of military service. The interpretation of the *dhimma* as a revocable contract is that adopted by Dr Mohamed El-Awa in his 'Note on Islam and other faiths' in this volume.

Chapter 3   Communities of faith

1   Surah 2.256.

2   Article 25, Constitution of Pakistan.

3   Articles 20 to 22, Constitution of Pakistan.

4   Surah 2.256.

5   Surah 10.99.

6   Surah 29.46.

7   Surah 22.40.

8   Surah 5.82.

9   Surah 60.8.

10   Surah 3.64.

11   Surah 2.62, 112; 5.69.

12   Surah 3.42.

13   Surah 3.19, 67; 4.125.

14   Surah 3.85.

15   Surah 29.46.

16   Justice A. R. Cornelius served as Pakistan's Chief Justice for over eight years, but such examples are rare.

17   On 17 January 2002, President Musharraf announced that the next national elections – scheduled for October that year – would be held under a restored joint electoral system, with the abandonment of separate seats reserved for minorities.

18   See Glossary.

19   See Glossary.

20   Section 295-C of the Penal Code.

21   Some commentators, for example, suggest that Surah 5.82 (cited by Dr Shah in his paper) has been abrogated by Surah 9.29: 'Fight those who believe not in Allah nor in the Last Day, nor forbid that which Allah and His Messenger have forbidden, nor follow the Religion of Truth out of those who have been given the Book.'

22   Emir Abdelkader to Mgr Antoine Pavy, unpublished letter of 1860. The emir was responding to a note from the bishop thanking him for his intervention to save the lives of thousands of Christians threatened with massacre in Damascus.

23   E.g. 'When freedom, out of a desire to emancipate itself from all forms of tradition and authority, shuts out even the most obvious evidence of an objective and universal truth, which is the foundation of personal and social life, then the person ends up by no longer taking as the sole and indisputable point of reference for his own choices the truth about good and evil, but only his subjective and changeable opinion or indeed, his selfish interest and whim. This view of freedom leads to a distortion of life in society. If the promotion of the self is understood in terms of absolute autonomy, people inevitably reach the point of rejecting one another. Everyone else is considered an enemy from whom one has to defend oneself. Thus society becomes a mass of individuals placed side by side, but without any mutual bonds.' John Paul II, *Evangelium Vitae*, English tr. (London: Catholic Truth Society, 1995) paras 19 and 20.

24   Augustine, *City of God*, tr. H. Bettenson (Penguin, 1972), xiv, 1.

25   O. M. T. O'Donovan, *The Desire of the Nations* (Cambridge University Press, 1996), pp. 83, 203.

26   Augustine, *City of God*, xiv, 28.

27   Augustine, *City of God.*, xiv, 1.

28   Augustine, *City of God.*, xix, 13.

29   Augustine, *City of God.*, xix, 12.

30   Of the imperial peace, Augustine exclaims (*City of God*, xix, 7): 'Think of the cost of this achievement! Consider the scale of those wars with all that slaughter of human beings, all the human blood that was shed!'

31   The prime mark of this injustice is the existence of slavery. According to Augustine (*City of God*, xix, 15), the proper relationship between human beings is 'prescribed by the order of nature, and it is in this situation that God created man. For he says, "Let him have lordship over the fish of the sea, the birds of the sky . . . and all the reptiles that crawl on the earth." He did not wish the rational being, made in his own image, to have dominion over any but irrational creatures, not man over man, but man over beasts. Hence the first just men were set up as shepherds of flocks, rather than as kings of men'.

32   In the midst of a melancholy review of the woes of life produced by division and conflict within house, city, world and even within that 'angelic fellowship' posited by 'those philosophers' who insist that 'the gods are our friends', Augustine notes (*City of God*, xix, 5) that the peace of the earthly city is 'a doubtful good, since we do not know the hearts of those with whom we wish to maintain peace, and even if we could know them today, we should not know what they might be like tomorrow.'

33   Leo XIII, *Rerum Novarum*, English tr. by the Catholic Truth Society (CTS, 1983), para. 37.

34   *Rerum Novarum.*, para. 38.

35   *Catechism of the Catholic Church* (Chapman, 1994), para. 1882, citing Mater et Magistra 60.

36   *Catechism*, 1882.

37   *Catechism*, 1879.

38   *Catechism*, 1699.

39   *Catechism*, 1711.

40   *Catechism*, 1878.

41   K. Barth, *Church Dogmatics*, III/2, eds G. Bromiley and T. F. Torrance. and tr. H. Knight et al. (T. & T. Clark, 1960), p. 243.

42   *Catechism*, 1183, citing *Centesimus Annus*.

43   *Catechism.*, 1184.

44   Luther, *On Secular Authority*, ed. and tr. H. Höpfl (Cambridge University Press, 1991), editor's introduction, p. xiii.

45   Luther, *On Secular Authority.*, p. xi.

46   *Barmen Declaration*, tr. D. S. Bax, *Journal of Theology for Southern Africa*, 47, 1984, I.

47   O'Donovan, *The Desire of the Nations*, p. 255.

48   O'Donovan, *The Desire of the Nations*, p. 252.

49   O'Donovan, *The Desire of the Nations*, p. 254.

50   Surah 22.30–31.

51   Many earlier Prophets are mentioned in the Qur'anic text itself; cf. Surahs 2.285 and 40.78.

52   Surahs 49.13, 4.1.

53   Surah 22.17.

54   Surah 2.62. – 'They shall not be afraid neither shall they be sad.'

55   Surah 16.125 – 'God knows who have strayed from his way and who are the well-guided.'

56   Surah 98.8. The immediately following verse orders Muslims to avoid supporting those who fight Muslims because of their religion, or who force them out of their homeland or ally with those who do so (98.9).

57   This principle is emphasized in many other Qur'anic injunctions, e.g. Surah 3.28, 4.144, 5.57, 58.2, 98.1.

58   Surah 5.5.

59   Surah 3.113-15.

60   Surah 5.82.

61   Surah 109.6. This is a principle even more applicable in the case of followers of divine religions, the *ahl al-kitāb* ('people of the book'). This expression is correctly understood to include Jews, Christians, Sabians, Magians, followers of Abraham and other book-receiving prophets, such as the Prophet David. The common elements among all these is that they originally believe in God, have a revealed book, and follow one of God's Prophets.

62   Such a view is reflected in the Statement issued in December 2001 by the Arab Team for Muslim–Christian Dialogue. This is a declaration by an alliance of believers of the duties they owe to strengthen national unity in countries composed of citizens of different religions.

Chapter 4   Faith and change

1   For an account of some of the leading eighteenth-century approaches to history and the lessons that were learnt by historians, philosophers, jurists and others in the period after the wars of religion see J. G. A. Pocock, *Barbarism and Religion*, vols 1 and 2 (Cambridge: Cambridge University Press, 1999). On the efforts in international law in a later period to create a more civilized world see Martti Koskenniemi, *The Gentle Civilizer of Nations. The Rise and Fall of International Law* (Cambridge University Press, 2001). Koskenniemi is especially concerned to learn from international law's successes and failures, and suggests that its 'fall' and widespread replacement by 'instrumentalism' has left the world poorly equipped to move towards a better global civil order. Yet his sharply perceptive history and analysis, which includes discussion of ethics, morality, norms, conscience, universality, interdependence, human rights, rationality, tradition, and natural law, is extraordinarily inattentive to religion. Islam, Christianity, even 'religion' do not appear in the index. Perhaps it is too much to hope that such inattention will become less common among Western academics after September 11.

2   For a study of civil society by an international team of contributors who cover historical and contemporary aspects of it in the West and in the Southern hemisphere see Sudipta Kaviraj and Sunil Khilnani, eds, *Civil Society: History and Possibilities* (Cambridge University Press, 2001).

3   The main focus of this seminar is on these three, but it is important to take into account at least three others: Judaism, China and India. These, together with Christianity and Islam, have in common the engagement with capitalism and the presence of long and still lively wisdom traditions.

4   For a perceptive summary of the Ecumenical Movement's history and significance (together with a short bibliography) see Geoffrey Wainwright's article in *The Oxford Companion to Christian Thought*, ed. Adrian Hastings et al. (Oxford University Press, 2000), pp. 189ff.

5   A new major feature of world Christianity which has so far had little to do with ecumenism is the Pentecostal–Charismatic movement – it is estimated at about 300 million and growing rapidly. Its main impact has not been in Europe, so it is outside the scope of this paper. It is a form of lively, popular religion that has often flourished in modern urban settings, and has learnt to practise and spread Christianity amidst rapid change. For a broad sociological account of Pentecostalism see David Martin, *Pentecostalism: The World Their Parish* (Blackwell, 2002).

6   Koskenniemi, in *The Gentle Civilizer of Nations* (see note 1), is a good example of this. He recognizes the weaknesses of all the secular attempts to meet the problems of international affairs and ends on a rather despairing note, while also ignoring the significance of the world's religions.

7   For a fuller discussion of this with reference to the types of Christian theology in the last two centuries see David F. Ford, ed., *The Modern Theologians: An Introduction to Christian Theology in the Twentieth Century* (Blackwell, 1997), especially the Introduction, in which a fuller account of a typology relevant to the present argument is given. Looking at the history of Christianity from the New Testament and the early Church and on through its later developments, I see there too the mainstream emphasis avoiding the two extremes described above.

8   I hope that, if Muslim participants agree on the wisdom of affirmation, judgement and transformation, they might offer an Islamic understanding of them, or analogous concepts.

9   For a perceptive historical, philosophical and theological treatment of this in the context of relations between religious traditions, see Nicholas Lash, *The Beginning and the End of 'Religion'* (Cambridge University Press, 1996) especially Part One 'A meeting-place for truth' and within that pp. 19ff. on 'Education from idolatry, and the purification of desire'.

10   For a clear statement of this see Dietrich Bonhoeffer, *Ethics* (Collins, 1964) especially Chapters 4 and 5.

11   The same holds for schools. The UK government's recent recognition of the desirability of more faith-based schools is an important landmark in affirming that Britain is a religious and secular society. In historical perspective this might later appear as a sign of official recognition (and by a political party that has had a militantly anti-religious secularist strand) that the assumption of a linear 'progress' from religious past to non-religious future is not only wrong but damaging and dangerous. The task now is to make sure that the way these schools are conceived embodies the lessons of history. One predictable reaction to September 11 was to condemn the whole idea because religions breed division and conflict. That 'either-religious-or-secular' line needs to be countered by a 'religious-and-secular' approach in which both religious communities and other parties show they have learnt from the best and worst in history.

12   For a fuller account of the relation of ultimate and penultimate see Bonhoeffer, *Ethics*, Chapter 4.

13   If I ask about areas in which Christians in Britain might have lessons to learn from Muslims, they would include: insistence on faith needing to relate to the whole of life; the shaping of life with the help of disciplines such as regular prayer times; alertness to over-assimilation, compromises and idolatries; importance of family life; wisdom about dealing with racism; honouring education and those who teach; global solidarity with fellow-worshippers; and generous almsgiving.

14   It is fascinating to trace how much each already owes to Jews and to Greeks. It may be that the present unprecedented availability of (and often engagement with) other traditions such as Hinduism, Buddhism, Confucianism, the modern natural and human sciences, and the arts of many cultures is an opportunity for enrichments, developments and joint learning among Christians and Muslims that would dwarf their debt to Judaism and Hellenism.

15   It is instructive that the Ecumenical Movement among Christians began as distinct movements (especially the missionary movement, Faith and Order, and Life and Work) whose coalition into the World Council of Churches has only ever been a very partial success.

16   E.g. Surah 37.6-9: 'We have decked the lower heaven with constellations. They guard it against rebellious devils, so that they may not listen in to those on high. Meteors are hurled at them from every side; then, driven away, they are consigned to an eternal scourge' (tr. Dawood). Cf. also Surah 67.5.

17   See the discussion in his work of Qur'anic exegesis, *al-Mizān*.

18   Nicholas Lash, *Change in Focus* (London, 1973), p. 59.

19   Cf. his *Reconstruction of Religious Thought in Islam* (Lahore, 1931).

20   Quoted in Hans Zirker, *Christentum und Islam: Theologische Verwandtschaft und Konkurrenz* (Patmos, 1992), p. 183, nn. 43 and 44. This note is heavily indebted to this and other works of Zirker.

21   Ernst-Wolfgang Böckenförde, *Staat-Gesellschat-Kirche*, in: CGG 15, pp. 5–120, here p. 16.

22   *Gaudium et Spes* [GS], art. 33.

23   GS, art. 33.

24   GS, art. 40.

25   GS, art. 44.

26   See: Christian W. Troll, 'Changing Catholic Views of Islam' in J. Waardenburg, ed., *Islam and Christianity: Mutual Perceptions since the Mid-twentieth Century* (Peeters, 1998) pp. 19–77; id., 'Catholic Teachings on Interreligious Dialogue: Analysis of some recent official documents, with special reference to Christian–Muslim relations' in J. Waardenburg, ed., *Muslim–Christian Perceptions of Dialogue Today* (Peeters, 2000) pp. 233–74.

27   London: Islamic Council, 1981/1401. The English and French versions of the text and a range of critical studies on the history, nature and relevance of the Muslim human rights declarations can be found in *Islamochristiana* (Rome), 9, 1983.

Chapter 5   Setting the agenda

1   Cf. the references in Acts – 9.2, 19.9, 19.23, 24.22.

2   T. S. Eliot, 'Journey of the Magi' (1937), in *Collected Poems, 1909–1962* (Faber, 1975), p. 110. Cf. Matt. 2.12: 'Having been warned in a dream not to return to Herod, they [the magi] left for their own country by another road.'

3   Martin Buber, tr. R. G. Smith, *I and Thou* (T. & T. Clark, 1937), p. 76.

4   'Story Water', in C. Barks and J. Moyne, ed. and tr., *The Essential Rumi* (Penguin, 1995).

5   M. Milner, A *Life of One's Own* (Chatto & Windus, 1934), p. 106.

6   Cf. the hadith, *Man arafa nafsahu faqd arafa rabbahu.* I am indebted to the Bishop of Rochester for this reference.

Index

Note: Page references in **bold** type are to items in the Glossary